CONTENTS

CATHEDRALS AND CASTLES
BUILDING IN THE MIDDLE AGES

Alain Erlande-Brandenburg

DISCOVERIES
HARRY N. ABRAMS, INC., PUBLISHERS

"As the third year that followed the year one thousand drew near, there was to be seen over almost all the earth, but especially in Italy and in Gaul, a great renewal of church buildings; each Christian community was driven by a spirit of rivalry to have a more glorious church than the others. It was as if the world had shaken itself, and, casting off its old garments, had dressed itself again in every part in a white robe of churches."

Raoul Glaber, *Historia*, c. 1003

CHAPTER I
A NEW WORLD

Gothic and Romanesque building sites are shown in detail in manuscript illuminations. The 15th-century picture opposite illustrates all the stages in building, from mixing the mortar to laying the tiles on the roof. Right: A temple under construction.

The Age of Pillaging and Sacking Came to an End

The raids of the Vikings, or Northmen (Normans), proved far more murderous and dramatic to Western Europeans than the barbarian invasions of the 5th century. Repeated onslaughts by well-disciplined troops tirelessly wending their way up streams and rivers brought havoc and devastation. Efforts to organize the Western Empire came to nothing due to sieges of towns and monasteries and the very heavy tribute that had to be paid to mount them. The treaty of St.-Clair-sur-Epte in 911, signed by a Viking leader and the Frankish king, granted to the Northmen a territory that soon became known as Normandy; it was to be a decisive factor in Western European history.

The destroyers settled down and became builders, founding an advanced national state before going on to conquer other lands in southern Italy and England. All of Europe was affected; from this time on it was involved on an extraordinary venture, which in the realm of architecture took on a decisively new character.

The Architectural Explosion of the Middle Ages

Ancient Egypt and Ancient Rome left a unique architectural heritage, the first over a long period of time and the second over a briefer span but a wider area. However, in both areas, great works appear as though created in isolation and not as a product of the general will.

Western Europe presents a different picture. There, architecture did not spring only from political power; it stemmed from all human beings, monks as well as politicians, peasants as well as lords. It involved all spheres: urban, administrative, financial, and

The development of larger sailing ships and longboats with oars —elegant, steady craft that did not draw much water (above left)— gave the Vikings great mobility and enabled them to carry out raids, even on horseback.

religious, in the town as well as in the country. At first the new buildings followed Roman forms, but they soon broke free. The defensive walls constructed in the 4th century to protect the old towns enclosed an inner area much too small to contain a rapidly expanding medieval population. Throughout the Middle Ages, alterations, improvements, and extensions continued to be made.

A New World

This society, which sought to affirm its destiny in stone, experienced a population explosion unprecedented in history, though it is difficult to give exact figures. It has been suggested that the population of Europe more than doubled between the 10th and

The population explosion of the early Middle Ages caused cities to burst beyond their defensive stone walls. Outside, suburbs grew up around religious centers, while vast areas remained entirely rural. Moulins, France, as it appeared in the second half of the 15th century (above), clearly illustrates this development.

the 14th centuries, rising from 14,700,000 around the year 600 to 22,600,000 in 950 and 54,400,000 before the Great Plague of 1348. According to other historians, the figure may have been as high as 73,000,000 at the beginning of the 14th century.

This population explosion was closely linked to two other factors, themselves inseparable: technological advances in agriculture and the growth of the town. The great extension of the area of cultivated land due to intensive clearing reached its peak in the first half of the 12th century; agricultural yield, even if relatively low by modern standards, doubled or even tripled, thanks to the three-year rotation of crops and the introduction of the asymmetrical plow, with a moldboard to turn the soil. Better tools, collars for draft animals, and the use of dung as fertilizer all help to explain this great advance, but it was neither regular nor systematic. There were striking differences between one region and another and between one landowner and another. The best yields were to be found on the lands belonging to the Cistercians, the monastic order founded by St. Bernard of Clairvaux.

The medieval town was no longer the city of the ancient world, the *urbs,* which was essentially political in nature and served to bring peoples together and blend conquerors and conquered. The medieval town was above all social. It sprang from the great earlier population centers, which

Representations of rural life tend to be as stylized as those of building sites. Four separate actions that happen at different times —plowing, sowing, harvesting, and threshing—are represented in one picture. In this illumination from the

beginning of the 15th century, the artist nevertheless includes technical details, such as the metal share and coulter on the moldboard of the otherwise wooden plow.

had been considerably altered in the 4th century when Rome ordered the enclosure of the administrative sector within mighty defensive walls. From *urbs* the town became *castrum* (a fortress),

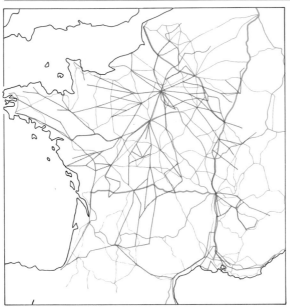

On a map of France, the juxtaposition of the road network created by the conquering Romans for strategic reasons (the fine blue lines) and the one built up in the 16th century (in red) emphasizes the revolution that took place in the country's infrastructure during the Middle Ages. New roads were created, bridges built, canals cut, and watercourses made navigable.

protecting the surrounding land, which was itself enclosed by a fortified boundary line, the *limes*.

The Medieval Town

The city wall sheltered the public buildings, which soon came to include the cathedral. Most of the population continued to live in the country. In the 10th century the *castrum* was all but abandoned by the civil authorities as well as the population; only the bishop continued to reside there,

ensuring permanence and looking after the few inhabitants. At Beauvais, texts speak of fifty households, about three hundred people. During the 11th century, this picture changed. Towns were born, or reborn, as a result of the influx of people the country could no longer feed or who were looking for wealth or adventure. A bond was to form between these people of such different backgrounds, leading to the formation of a kind of urban upper class.

Once established, this partnership tended to make the towns both economically and commercially active. The town/country relationship was reversed, with the latter now working for the former. Towns became markets and meeting places, thereby creating a network of commercial links. Then came systems of communication by land or by water: Roads were built, supplementing the Roman military routes. This new network was molded by the needs of commerce and the nature of the topography. As for waterways, the development of many large rivers

I nside ramparts that had been newly constructed or adapted from earlier structures, as in the amphitheater at Arles (left), urban and rural activities could take place side by side (above). There might, for instance, be a whole area devoted to stock raising, which ensured permanent provisions. Starting in the 15th century, building in stone began to be the norm for the houses of the nobility.

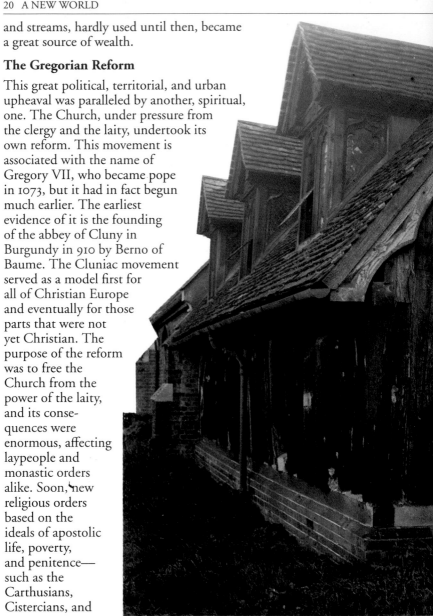

and streams, hardly used until then, became
a great source of wealth.

The Gregorian Reform

This great political, territorial, and urban
upheaval was paralleled by another, spiritual,
one. The Church, under pressure from
the clergy and the laity, undertook its
own reform. This movement is
associated with the name of
Gregory VII, who became pope
in 1073, but it had in fact begun
much earlier. The earliest
evidence of it is the founding
of the abbey of Cluny in
Burgundy in 910 by Berno of
Baume. The Cluniac movement
served as a model first for
all of Christian Europe
and eventually for those
parts that were not
yet Christian. The
purpose of the reform
was to free the
Church from the
power of the laity,
and its conse-
quences were
enormous, affecting
laypeople and
monastic orders
alike. Soon, new
religious orders
based on the
ideals of apostolic
life, poverty,
and penitence—
such as the
Carthusians,
Cistercians, and

Between the 9th and the 12th centuries a technique of building developed using vertical planks, which were tied together. The wall was thus made up of jointed elements. The technique evolved into two types differentiated by the presence or absence of corner posts. The south wall of the church at Greenstead in Essex, England (far left), belongs to the first group. (The rest of the building was built later.) Inside, posts support the roof. By this time, major buildings were already being constructed in stone.

A drawing from the 1060s (above) depicts the consecration of an Anglo-Saxon cathedral, perhaps Wells. The draftsman took care to show the lower part of the walls and the tower as built of squared stones, or ashlar, emphasizing the joints.

Premonstratensians—were created.

Western Europe was thus transformed to create a more just and more ambitious modern world, in which everyone would find a place in one of three new classes: those who fought, those who prayed, and those who worked. This break with the Carolingian era was based upon an unprecedented mastery of technology, which found its supreme expression in the realm of architecture.

Stone vs. Wood

New requirements confronted society in the 11th century. Architecture had to be rethought in the light of hitherto-unknown demands. These came from the administrative sphere, with the new road system, which entailed the building of many bridges; from the military sphere, with the struggle of great or lesser lords to maintain or extend their might and power; and from the religious sphere, with the need to receive larger congregations in cathedrals and parish churches and to ensure the life of prayer of monks in new monasteries withdrawn from the world. A taste for comfort and space became evident at the same time. Until now, all building had been of wood, except for the most important monuments, such as those concerned with worship. Now, little by little, wood gave way to stone, unevenly but surely. The mason gradually took the place of the carpenter.

Stone replaced wood in military architecture. The earthen motte was topped at first by a wooden keep, and later by one in stone. The design remained faithful to the original, with a square ground plan, dominating height, and few openings.

The Feudal Motte

In early times fortresses of earth and wood were raised throughout a large part of Europe. No specialized knowledge was

needed to erect these structures. The earth excavated from a circular moat was piled up in the center to form a mound, or motte, varying in height

Above: The motte and keep of Albon in southeastern France.

and diameter. Then a wooden tower was erected on the top. The sloping sides of the motte were protected by thornbushes, the barbed wire of the time. This was not a very effective means of protection, as several scenes in the famous 11th-century Bayeux Tapestry indicate, for the bushes could easily be set on fire by burning missiles.

Stone Defenses

The development of residential architecture is striking proof of the growth of building in stone.

This technical advance was closely linked to the desire for increased defenses. Starting in the middle of the 11th century, chroniclers drew attention to the use of masonry, and this became the norm in the next century.

The feudal motte, which was easy to construct, was a familiar part of the landscape of Western Europe. It could be seen from a long way away. The Bayeux Tapestry, which relates the conquest of England in 1066 by William, Duke of Normandy, gives several examples of mottes, in particular in the episode on the attack on the town of Rennes (opposite), where the motte was scaled by means of a wooden ladder. Mottes under siege were surrounded on all sides (above). If the keep was made of wood, attackers tried to set it on fire; if it was of stone, they tried to conquer the defenders by starvation.

Nevertheless, the first stone castles were built in the rectangular shape of the wooden fortresses. This was due not only to conservatism: They had specific functions—to serve as dwelling places and to contain the great state room or hall as well as the living rooms—so both their shape and their size were determined by their function, at ground level and above.

In the mid-12th century, when the lords left for more comfortable dwellings, the towers took on a purely defensive character. Their rectangular plan was abandoned in favor of a circular one (as at Provins, Houdan, Etampes, and elsewhere).

From 1190, the French king Philip Augustus' architects popularized the idea of the cylindrical tower, an idea occasionally copied in England, as at Conisbrough in Yorkshire. Wood had by then been almost entirely replaced by stone. There were stone spiral staircases inside the walls, stone-vaulted rooms, and a flat stone roof serving as a platform, sometimes accompanied by a corbeled-out wooden gallery so that the foot of the walls could be watched.

Bridges, Roads, and Technical Feats

This transition from wood to stone also appeared in the civic sphere. In the Carolingian era (8th–10th centuries), in contrast to the ancient world, bridges were usually made of timber. The bridge over the Rhine, built by Eginhard at Charlemagne's request, was made of wood. When it burned down in 813, a replacement made of stone was considered. The project was abandoned after Charlemagne's death and never resumed. Many Carolingian texts mention such wooden constructions, designed to make streams and rivers impassable to Viking boats, while at the same time enabling civilians and soldiers to cross. That dual purpose would last for the greater part of the Middle Ages.

It was fairly easy to build a wooden bridge, and the work, which could be accomplished quite quickly, required relatively few skilled craftsmen (opposite). This was still the case when the Allied army landed in Europe in 1944.

A drawing by Villard de Honnecourt—a rare survival from the 13th century—shows a fifty-five-foot-long bridge, apparently built to cross a mountain river. A timber roadway structure is held between the stone abutments. Stone bridges were intended to be permanent, and technical mastery was needed to make them resistant to air and water.

In order to promote the new commercial network, many bridges were begun during the 11th century, as parts of schemes linking one estate to another. Bishop Arnaud I, who wanted to make his cathedral at Maguelonne near Montpellier more accessible, built

The bridge of Gour-Noir (left), which spans the Hérault River in France, was constructed around 1030. Built of small coursed stones characteristic of that period, it already has side openings to allow floodwater to pass through.

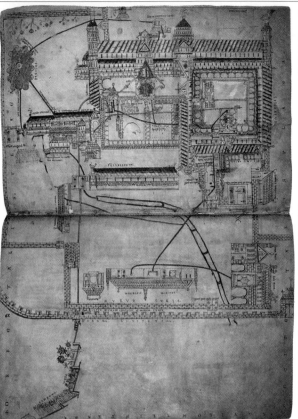

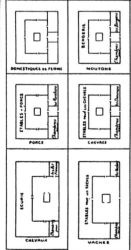

The 1150s plan at left shows the water circulation system for the monastery of Christchurch, Canterbury.

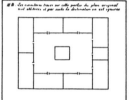

PLAN DE SAINT-GALL
(IX° Siècle)

N.B. *Les caractères tracés sur cette partie du plan original sont oblitérés et par suite la destination en est ignorée*

ENTRÉE COMMUNE

DOMESTIQUES de FERME	BERGERIE MOUTONS
ÉTABLES à PORCS PORCS	ÉTABLES pour les CHÈVRES CHÈVRES
ÉCURIE CHEVAUX	ÉTABLES pour les VACHES VACHES

BÂTIMENTS de FERME

a bridge over a half-mile long across the marshes.

All these bridges were still of wood, and it is difficult to give a precise date for the first stone bridge. It seems likely that at first only the piers were of stone and that they supported a wooden superstructure. Such superstructures were easy to construct, but they were relatively fragile and could be swept away in a flood. What's more, they were not well suited to heavy traffic. Architects clearly turned to Roman models, of which many survived. By the end of the 13th century, bridges were commonly built of stone, with solidly grounded piers and designs that took wind- and water resistance into account. To make provision for exceptionally high floods, holes were even built at a higher level to let the river through. The surviving medieval bridges at Cahors and Avignon both show the engineers' concern for this danger, which was something new.

Monastic Architecture

Churches in monasteries had always been built of stone, though the nave might be roofed in wood.

At the beginning of the 9th century, an unexecuted plan for the reconstruction of the abbey of St. Gall in Switzerland (below) attempted to organize and reconcile the worldly and the spiritual life. The designer relied on the ancient principle of *insulae* (islands), here centered on the church.

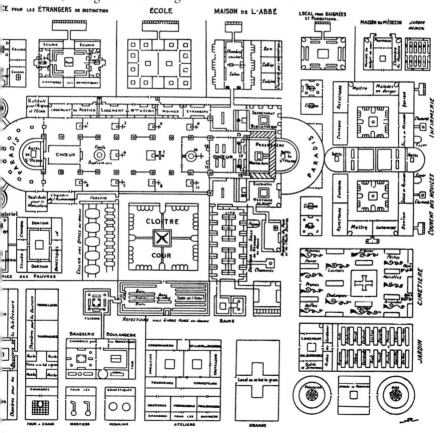

The famous St. Gall plan, a drawing from the early 9th century depicting an ideal monastery, shows out-buildings constructed of wood with an abbey church of stone. In the 11th century, outbuildings were already found in stone, such as the famous stables at Cluny built by the abbot St. Hugh. During the 12th century monastic buildings came to be constructed entirely of stone, a change that gradually worked its way down from the most important buildings to the most humble.

Cistercian barns of the 12th and 13th centuries illustrate this generalization. These huge buildings consist of a stone exterior divided into nave and aisles either by wooden posts (Froidement) or by stone piers (Maubuisson).

Expanding Towns and New Fortifications

Finally came urban architecture. In the 15th century, the usual formula for dwellings was a stone ground floor and timber upper stories, but even before then facades made entirely of stone were to be found. There are impressive 12th-century examples at Cluny, as well as at the upper town of Provins and at Viviers. The 12th century also saw the construction of

The construction of a tower, using very simple wooden scaffolding, from a French manu-script of the 13th century.

particularly large new schemes of defensive walls. The early walls proved too small to contain an expanding population. Sometimes the new walls enclosed a new urban entity, consisting of the old walled town, the suburbs, and several outlying areas of settlement (as at Toulouse, Arras, Limoges, and Paris). Here too, stone replaced fortifications made of wood. There is evidence of this fact in 1137 when Eudes III erected an enclosing wall at Dijon about one and a half miles long. However, it was Paris (Notre-Dame) that set the pattern. King Philip Augustus built city walls, first on the right bank of the Seine (1190), then on the left bank (1210), taking in an area of 625 acres.

All these walls were admirably constructed in stone. From this period on, large, mid-sized, and small towns were all surrounded by ramparts whose purpose was not just to provide protection.

The stone ramparts of the upper town of Provins are almost complete. They follow the contours of the land and are punctuated by semicircular or multifaceted defensive towers. A steep slope protected the foundations from being undermined.

They also united scattered settlements and promoted a sense of identity within the town. In some cities these new walls were quickly outgrown, and new, much larger ones had to be constructed. King Charles V enclosed the right bank of Paris—an area of about 1080 acres comprising the commercial, rich quarter—within a new wall, making the city the most populous in Europe.

At the end of the Middle Ages towns were composed of several urban units joined inside a wall whose purpose was as much psychological as defensive. From these disparate units a new community arose.

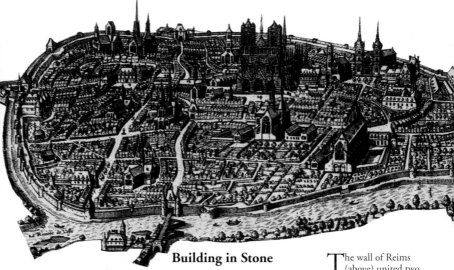

Building in Stone

The adoption of stone was not without difficulties. Stone cost more; working it required skilled masons; it had to be found and transported to the site; and to

The wall of Reims (above) united two towns: the ancient city, at the left, around the cathedral, and the suburb of St.-Remi, around the abbey at the right.

There is a link between the rapid expansion of cities and the ever-increasing size of cathedrals. Cathedrals' importance was emphasized by their expanding size. On the skyline, high civic and ecclesiastical towers became a city's emblems.

build with it required more sophisticated technology. To these inherent difficulties the fashion for colossal buildings soon had to be added.

Prague is a good—if extreme—example. The ruler of Bohemia sought to make his capital the seat of the Holy Roman Empire,

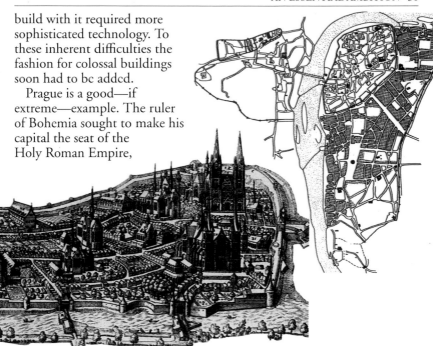

to shift the political center of a somewhat uncohesive body toward the east. In 1348, Emperor Charles IV founded a new city on the right bank of the Vltava River, which wrapped around the old town. He built huge streets that were sometimes as much as 82 feet wide, and 1650 houses, all of stone. Everything was enclosed by an 11,500-foot-long wall. The emperor also founded fifteen parish churches to satisfy the needs of a population of 85,000 inhabitants, and he established a huge marketplace and a town hall. What was remarkable for this time and place was the determination to build in nothing but stone. The new cathedral was begun by a French master mason, Matthew of Arras.

The Emperor's motives were much the same as those of President Juscelino Kubitschek when in 1957

In Prague (plan above), the castle and the Old Town, surrounded by Charles IV's New Town, were linked by the Charles Bridge (opposite below).

he launched the construction of Brasilia, a new capital for Brazil, and called on Oscar Niemeyer, one of the great architects of the time.

Vast New Cathedrals

This love for the colossal, which calls to mind large modern urban projects, did not apply to whole towns, but extended only to individual buildings. From the beginning of the Gothic era, no one dreamed of building a cathedral less than three hundred feet long. Height also became breathtaking. At Beauvais the distance from floor to vault is 155 feet; at Strasbourg the spire is 466 feet high.

This preference for the colossal was also present in parish

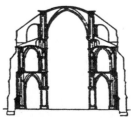

churches, some so large that they became cathedrals, when a diocese was subdivided and a new cathedral —its principal church—was needed. Church builders displayed the same ambition everywhere in Europe, from Ulm in the Holy Roman Empire to S. Maria del Mar in Barcelona, built by shipowners and merchants who sought to compete with the largest buildings of the time and entrusted the project to Berenguer de Montagut in 1328. The same was true of Cistercian abbeys, such as Foigny, 320 feet long, and Vaucelles, 433 feet long. Some monasteries were as big as towns; Fontevrault, for example, was divided into four districts around the great church and the churches of St. Mary Magdalen, St. Lazarus, and St. John. In England, the Cistercians were equally active— Fountains and Rievaulx in Yorkshire—and in some of the older abbeys the abbot also functioned as a bishop, as at Canterbury. And municipal architecture in no way lagged behind when it came to size. For example, the 14th-century Charles Bridge across the Vltava in Prague is 1683 feet long.

Diversity and Dissemination

It is difficult to estimate today what this architectural activity of the Middle Ages represented. Many buildings have disappeared, some of them a long time ago. Surviving defensive architecture, though

Stone fostered the human dream of erecting ever-higher buildings. The Tower of Babel is the most common illustration of that dream in the Middle Ages, but there were other images. In a drawing by Jan van Eyck (opposite right), the tower, symbolic of St. Barbara, serves as a pretext to represent a masons' lodge.

The reality of Gothic buildings bears witness to this enthusiasm for size, whose growing audacity is seen in the increasing height of cathedral nave vaults: 79 feet at Laon around 1160, 121 feet at Chartres in 1194, and 153 feet at Beauvais in 1225 (opposite and below, left to right).

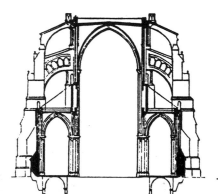

eloquent, is only the ghost of an extraordinary reality to which texts and pictures bear witness. Europe is covered with important buildings, some of which are decisive in the history of architecture. While the area around Paris was to gain and keep architectural dominance in France, in England there were a number of centers of equal importance—London, Canterbury, York, Lincoln, and Bristol.

There is no disputing the conclusions to be drawn. "In a period of three centuries, from 1050 to 1350, several million tons of stone were quarried in France for the building of eighty cathedrals, five hundred large churches, and some tens of thousands of parish churches. More stone was

Illuminators in the Middle Ages tried to render the finer details of topography not by perspective but by placing views of different distances one above the other, as in this portrayal of four cities (left).

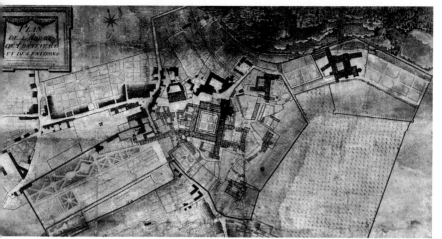

moved in France during these three centuries than at any time in ancient Egypt, although the volume of the Great Pyramid alone is 2,500,000 cubic meters [3,267,500 cubic yards]." This statement from Jean Gimpel's *The Cathedral Builders* (1959) has lost none of its relevance. More recent histories of medieval architecture have taken account not only of religious but also of civil, military, and municipal architecture. The overall picture has thereby been considerably enriched.

A 15th-century drawing of Montaigut-le-Blanc, in south-central France (left), successfully suggests the slope of the land, and conveys the dominant impact of the tower.

The 18th-century architect who drew the plans of the abbey of Fontevrault (above) was interested in the layout of the various buildings on the ground, not in their effect on the viewer.

"A building will never be worthy if the architect is unworthy." Thus said a late-12th-century king of France when asking an abbot to recommend an architect. The architect was an intellectual, a man possessed of *scientia*, or specialized knowledge, a master builder—never, under any circumstances, a mere executor of a task, trained on the building site.

CHAPTER II
THE ARCHITECT

Hugues Libergier, architect of St.-Nicaise at Reims (d. 1263), is depicted on his tombstone holding a model of the building and dressed in clothes that showed his high social standing. The rod, the set square, and the dividers are the indications of his profession.

Until the 11th century architectural activity sprang from a royal court. The sovereign, whether king or emperor, was the prime patron. However, the new era, the Middle Ages, which continued up to the dawn of the Renaissance, is characterized by the diversity of patrons. This explains both its extraordinary richness and its no less extraordinary variety. The sovereign certainly continued to play a leading role, but he dominated his own sphere, in matters concerning palaces or defense works. Some did not hesitate to go beyond that, building or planning whole towns, like the Emperor Charles IV in Prague and King Charles V in Paris in the 14th century, but this function was largely taken over by the clergy—bishops, abbots, or canons—and by the laity—lords, communities, cities, and associations. The sheer number of patrons was thus greatly increased.

The Patron and the Genesis of the Project

At the same time, a close relationship grew up between patron and architect (also called a master mason), working in concert to bring a complex, ambitious enterprise to completion.

The patrons were naturally decisive in the creation of a building. They originated the projects and had to provide the funds. They chose the architects and ensured the continuity of the works. A patron's death usually caused a crisis: Work might slow down, stop

The relationship between patron and architect was based on trust. Artists understood this very well and depicted them on an equal footing. In this 13th-century drawing (above left), the king who had built St. Albans Abbey is shown talking to his architect.

In a stained-glass window from St.-Germer-de-Fly (above), Abbot Pierre de Wessencourt is talking to his architect in the presence of some stonecutters and laborers.

Left: The miniaturist who illustrated a celebrated Latin work on rural life by Petrus Crescentius shows how to build a house in the country under the joint instructions of master mason and patron.

completely, or there might be a change in the plan. The death of Abbot Suger in 1151 stopped the rebuilding of the abbey church of St.-Denis at once; work was not resumed until almost a century later, in 1231, when it took a totally different course.

The initiation of large construction projects was linked, as it is nowadays, to the presence of visionaries, whose ambition sometimes provoked violent negative reactions from those involved in the budgets for the enterprises. Over all these buildings hovers the shadow of exceptional individuals. Some were bishops, such as Fulbert of Chartres at the beginning of the 11th century or Maurice de Sully in Paris in 1160; some were abbots, such as William of Volpiano at St.-Bénigne at Dijon, and Notre-Dame at Bernay at the beginning of the 11th century; some were kings, such as Philip Augustus in the 12th century or Frederick II in the 13th century; some were great lords, such as Fulk Nerra, count of Anjou; and some were urban communities, such as Florence, Milan, and Siena. Without the patrons' strength of purpose, cathedrals, castles, town halls, and bridges would never have come into existence. The construction of these structures was an architectural manifestation of piety, indispensable to the life of society, its flowering, and its happiness.

Building was also a display of temporal power. Eudes, count of Blois, ordered a bridge to be built over the Loire at Blois in 1033. In that same year, the chapter of Albi Cathedral was compelled to build a bridge, but in return obtained the lordship of it. The consuls of Cahors began the Pont-Neuf in 1251 and the Pont Valentré in 1306. In Florence, Orvieto, and Siena, it was the commune that took charge of the cathedral. A lord hoping to atone for his sins might found a hospital. The different origins of the patrons serves to explain numerous problems.

The relationship between patron and architect was founded on a clear and precise document. Contracts were common by the 13th century. When Hans Hammer was engaged at Strasbourg Cathedral in 1486, a text was drawn up on parchment (below), and five seals were appended: those of the Oeuvre Notre-Dame (the fabric committee), the knight Hans Rudolf von Endingen, the *Altammeister* Peter Schott, the administrator Andreas Haxmacher, and the receiver of the Oeuvre, Conrad Hammelburger. The last

Huge Stakes

The realization of the facade of Strasbourg Cathedral went through many changes of plan, due to continuing tension between the bishop and the city, which the contract of 1263 in no way diminished. The first four men were signatories to the contract. Hans Hammer designed the cathedral pulpit, among other things.

design was abandoned, as often happened in the 13th and 14th centuries. The city would not allow itself to be excluded from the construction site, which was a symbol of civic pride. In Siena the population of the city undertook the construction of the new cathedral, a circumstance that expressed itself in changes of plan and interruptions. In Milan, the *fabbrica*, or fabric committee—which concerned itself with the construction and maintenance of church buildings—grew from 105 members in 1387 to nearly 300 in 1401, making decisions difficult. This process of democratization, which began in cathedral building in the first third of

The construction of Reims Cathedral (below) must certainly have involved contracts, although they have not come down to us. The facade was begun after 1225 by an architect who drastically modified the original project, replacing it with a design that was more in the style of his time.

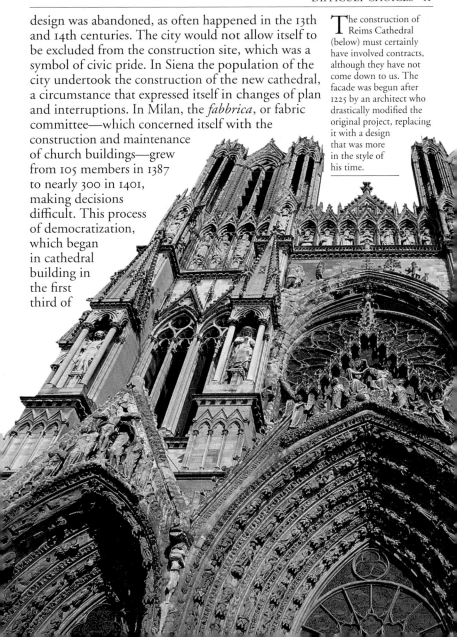

the 13th century, was generally linked to financial difficulties, which could be lessened if there was common consent.

The patron, whether an individual, a community, or an association, was responsible for commissioning the architect after describing the project to him. At the end of the 10th century and the beginning of the 11th, the patron often had to face the hard fact that there were few professionals available to respond to the challenge. Great architecture could not be created by architects with no more than local experience. Whereas in Carolingian times there had been trained architects, they no longer existed, because ambitious building projects had disappeared. Everything had to be learned again.

This explains the special position of many patrons: They were forced to become architects themselves to realize their vast plans. They challenged fate and demanded the utmost of everyone. They were clergy, bishops, or abbots, intellectuals familiar with antiquity and its monuments, with which they sought to compete. They looked to those ancient structures as models for themselves and for the architects they wanted to convince. The architectural scene, one must remember, was very

When King Solomon built the Temple (below), he is said to have employed nearly 200,000 workmen. The builder of Bourges Cathedral (opposite) had a more limited workforce and also created something astonishing.

different from today's. Many large ancient monuments still survived, dating from the early years of the Holy Roman Empire or even from late antiquity. By their very presence and their resistance to the ravages of time, they offered assurance that audacity could succeed.

Men of the Church

Gauzlin, Morard, William of Volpiano, and many others were powerful and active stimulating presences in the actual building process. There are revealing documents about Gauzlin at St.-Benoît-sur-Loire, which show him after the devastating fire of 1026: He ordered a tower to be built in stone that had to be transported some distance by water. His demands made problems but he succeeded in resolving them.

Such patrons demanded sharply jointed ashlar, not rubble roughly broken by hammers, which was widely accepted. At Auxerre in 1023 the chronicler was enraptured with these *quadris lapidibus* (squared stones). The same patrons were also responsible for developing new types of cathedral design, including one in which the ambulatory—the path around the apse—had radiating chapels, seen in the cathedrals of Rouen, Chartres, and Auxerre; it was soon to extend throughout ecclesiastical architecture, though England remained faithful to the square east end.

This picture glorifies William of Wykeham (1324–1404), a great patron at the end of the 14th century. The artist wishes to show the key role of an ambitious patron who knows how to find architects of great talent. Bishop of Winchester, founder of New College, Oxford, and of Winchester College, he imposed his own style on the buildings for which he was responsible.

After the Norman Conquest, intellectuals like Gundulf, who became bishop of Rochester in 1077, took things in hand. He was said to be "very learned and effective in the matter of building," and was entrusted with the reconstruction of Rochester Cathedral, as well as a monastery for sixty monks and many other works. In the 12th century, Hildebert, archbishop of Tours, himself measured foundations and decided on the dimensions of the palace.

A manuscript by the monk André de Mici depicts the new cathedral of Chartres, begun by Bishop Fulbert (1007–28) and completed by his successor, Thierry, in 1037. It was later replaced by the present Gothic building, but the old crypt still exists. In the upper part of the picture, the building is shown from the side, with the facade on the left and the chevet—the east end, with the apse—on the right. Below, we are looking down the nave flanked by aisles.

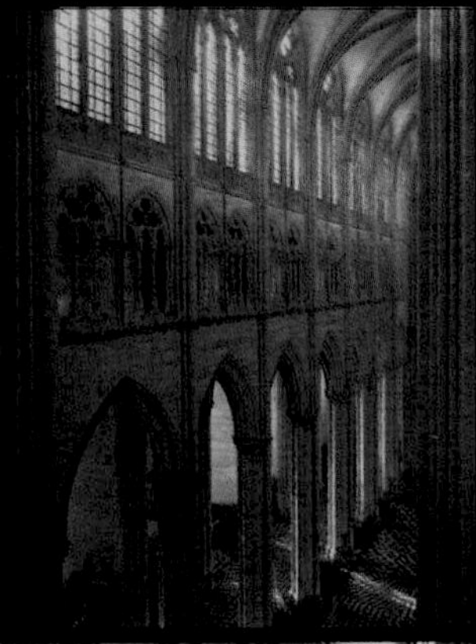

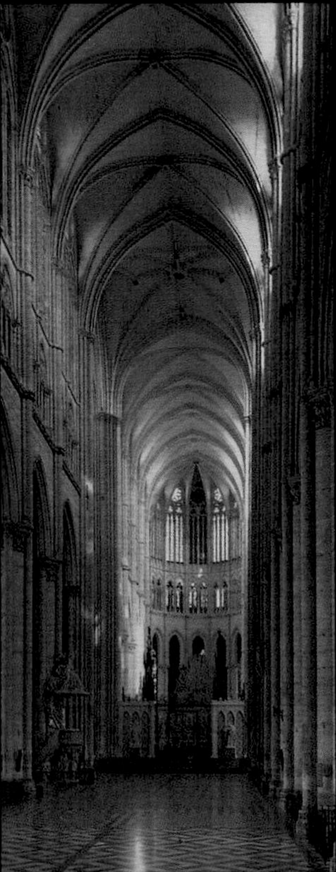

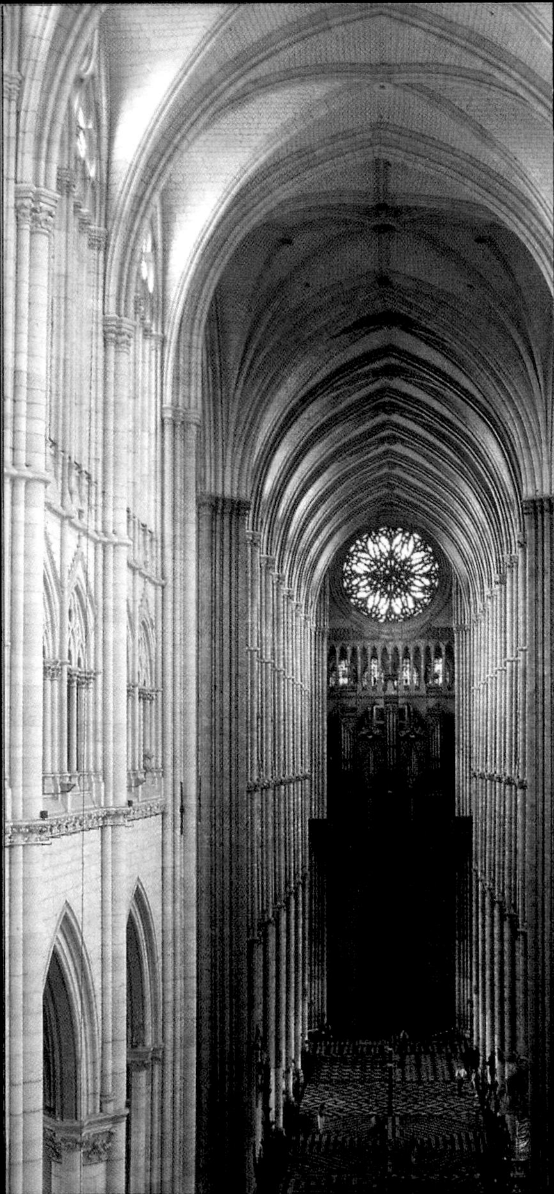

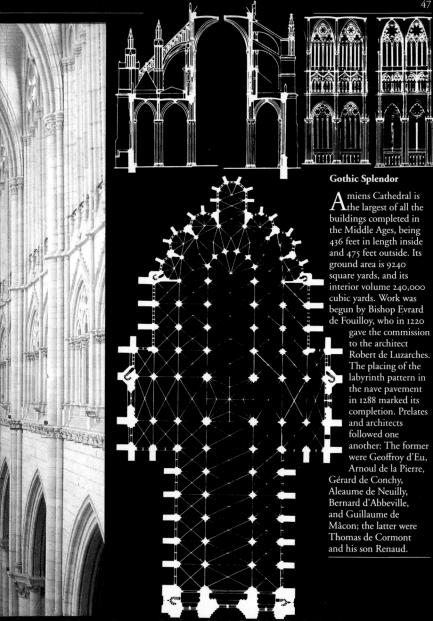

Gothic Splendor

Amiens Cathedral is the largest of all the buildings completed in the Middle Ages, being 436 feet in length inside and 475 feet outside. Its ground area is 9240 square yards, and its interior volume 240,000 cubic yards. Work was begun by Bishop Evrard de Fouilloy, who in 1220 gave the commission to the architect Robert de Luzarches. The placing of the labyrinth pattern in the nave pavement in 1288 marked its completion. Prelates and architects followed one another: The former were Geoffroy d'Eu, Arnoul de la Pierre, Gérard de Conchy, Aleaume de Neuilly, Bernard d'Abbeville, and Guillaume de Mâcon; the latter were Thomas de Cormont and his son Renaud.

The Glory of the Virgin

Impressive sculpted decoration was added to the vast stone structure of Amiens Cathedral. It remains intact on the exterior. The sculpture concentrates on the Virgin, to whom the cathedral was dedicated. The facade received the most attention, with the Last Judgment portal in the center, flanked on the south by the portal of the Mother of God, and on the north by the portal of St. Firmin. There are over-lifesize figures of apostles and prophets in the porches and in front of the buttresses, with quatrefoils of the labors of the months beneath and the kings of Judah along an upper gallery. On the south transept, the famous Vierge Dorée (Golden Virgin) occupies the trumeau (central post) of the portal, while the jambs are dedicated to St. Honoratus, the first bishop of Amiens.

In the meantime, however, professional architects had emerged. It became the norm to call on experts, and members of the clergy, such as Raymond Gayrard at St.-Sernin at Toulouse, began to confine themselves to the administration of the project.

Administration was itself no easy task, and it called for particular skills. The Cistercians acquired a reputation in this field. They included such men as Raoul at St.-Jouin de Marnes, who eventually became abbot of the monastery; St. Bernard's own brother, Achard, master of the novices, who supervised the construction of many monasteries, among them Himmerod in the Rhineland in 1134; Geoffrey d'Aignay, who was sent

Above: The Cistercian abbey of Schönau in Germany under construction.

PONTIFICI SVMMO CLAVSTRVM OFFERT CONCIO PATRVM,
VT FOVEAT IVGI PAPA BEATVS OPE.

to Fountains Abbey in Yorkshire in 1133; and Robert, to Mellifont in Ireland in 1142. John, a monk from La Trinité at Vendôme, was loaned by his abbot to the bishop of Le Mans, Hildebert de Lavardin, and when his task was over, he refused to return to his monastery.

The Modern Architect

As projects became more and more complex, it became imperative for the various tasks to be divided between specialists. It was during the second half of the 11th century that the architect established himself in the modern sense as one who, when so ordered by a patron, drew up the project, designed it, and was responsible for seeing it carried out. There was no hesitation in

A dominant characteristic of the 12th century was professionalism. The Cistercians played a prominent role through concern for economy and profitability. Unlike the monks of Cluny, who were more preoccupied with intellectual life, the Cistercians regarded manual work as a form of prayer. The manuscript of *Moralia in Job* by Gregory the Great, written and illustrated at Cîteaux in 1111 at the instigation of Abbot Stephen Harding, sent a clear message with its depiction of the various kinds of work carried out by the monks (opposite below, woodcutters). Starting in the beginning of the 14th century, the Cistercians promulgated a distinct image of their monasteries, spread at the end of the 15th century by means of woodcuts. Above: St. Robert of Molesmes, St. Aubin, and St. Stephen Harding present a model of Cîteaux to the pope. The monastery is depicted at the bottom, protected by a high wooden fence.

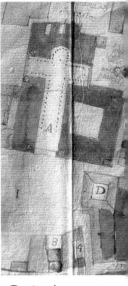

citing him by name; we know, for instance, that Gautier de Coorland was chosen by Emma, Queen of England and wife of William the Conqueror, to reconstruct St.-Hilaire at Poitiers.

The architects of the next generation, of the last third of the 11th century, dared to go in for especially ambitious enterprises at the patron's command. Until then, buildings with particularly wide naves, such as Jumièges and St. Albans Cathedral, were roofed in wood; St.-Martin du Canigou was stone vaulted, but it was less than 12 feet wide. Vaulting now began to span naves like that of St.-Sernin in Toulouse, 26 feet wide and 69 feet high, or Durham Cathedral. At the same time,

Santiago de Compostela owes its existence to the pilgrimage that drew crowds of worshipers anxious to honor the body of St. James, the holy apostle of Christ, which had miraculously been discovered in this corner of Spain at the time of Charlemagne. King Alfonso II at once built a church, and the town grew up around it (above). In 1183 the cathedral was rebuilt by Master Mateo, who created the celebrated Portico de la Gloria (left): St. James on the trumeau is flanked by apostles and prophets; above in the tympanum is Christ the Judge.

in contrast to ancient Roman architecture, these heavy vaults rested on slim supports. This was doubly experimental, and there were some accidents: A vault collapsed at Cluny in 1120, but the original plan had been to roof the abbey church with wood. It is easy to understand how fascinated people must have been with these men who seemed to defy all the accepted rules of building. Many written sources provide evidence for this.

The Evidence of History

Aimery Picaud, the author of the most famous medieval text relating to pilgrimage, a guide for pilgrims going to Santiago de Compostela called the *Liber Sancti Jacobi*, written between 1139 and 1173, takes care to mention the designer of the church: "The stone masons who undertook the construction of the church were Master Bernard the Elder—an inspired craftsman—and Robert, with the assistance of about another fifty lapicides [stonecutters] who all worked actively under the direction of Don Wicart,

A 13th-century manuscript depicts a meeting between patron and architect. To King Alfonso VIII and his wife, Alienor, both of them seated, Master Ferrandi (Pedro Fernández) is presenting the facade of the castle of Uclés, which the king gave around 1170–5 to the Knights of Santiago.

Master of the Chapter of Segeredo, and the abbot Don Gundesindo, in the reign of Alfonso, King of Spain, and of Diego I, a valiant cavalier and generous man." The decision to rebuild had been made in 1077, and the work started on 11 July 1078. The time taken to set up the workshop shows the difficulties encountered in a country where no enterprise on such a large scale had been attempted before. We know nothing about Bernard the Elder, except that recently it has been claimed that he had previously built bridges; it has generally been suggested that he was trained in France because of the French character of the church plan. He did not come on his own, but had with him fifty craftsmen who could cut stones, not merely break them with a hammer as was usual in the region. Robert presumably acted as the site architect, while the master of the chapter and Gundesindo administered the project, copying organizational methods that had worked elsewhere.

In the 12th century we find architects were mentioned more frequently and with more flattering comparisons. The architect Garin, in Verdun after 1131, was said to be more learned than his colleagues and compared to Hiram of Tyre, the builder of the Temple of Solomon. Their reputation was such that jealousy was aroused. It is said that the countess of Bayonne had the architect who had just built a tower at Pithiviers beheaded, lest he should repeat the exploit for another patron.

The First Gothic Architecture

Might jealousy explain the general anonymity that veils the architects of the early Gothic period? Perhaps their fame competed with that of the patron. The case of Abbot Suger of St.-Denis is particularly striking in

Abbot Suger was an active patron during the reconstruction of the Carolingian abbey church of St.-Denis. His death in 1151 meant that the nave that was to have joined the west end of the church to the apse remained unfinished. Proud of his work, Suger had himself represented in a stained-glass window in the apse, in a mosaic in one of the chapels (below), and in a sculpture at the feet of Christ on the central portal—each time in an attitude of profound humility. The basilica marked a break with the Romanesque tradition; the ambulatory (opposite), with its pointed arches and fine moldings, is a manifesto of the new Gothic style.

this respect. He diligently reported in the minutest detail everything about the reconstruction of his abbey church, while taking care not to mention the name of his architect. Was he trying to take the credit for the revolutionary construction of the choir, which was to usher in a new style? His silence was deliberate. Nothing was to tarnish his own glory, which he enhanced with many portraits of himself, even though by this point the professional role of the architect was in fact well established.

In 1175 the bishop and canons of Urgell signed a contract with Raymond the Lombard to complete their cathedral. With four other Lombards he undertook within the space of seven years to finish the work, which involved vaulting the church, erecting belltowers, and building a dome.

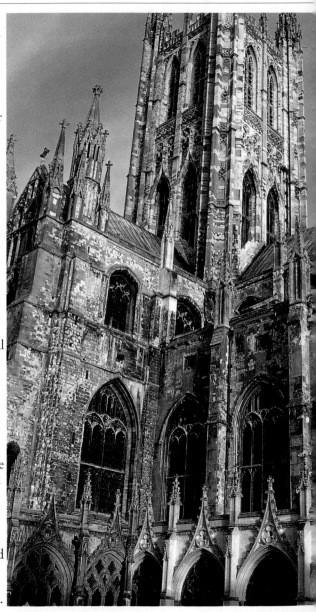

A written contract now became the norm, not only in ecclesiastical architecture but in military architecture as well. When Robert III Gateblé, count of Dreux, wanted to build the castle of Danemarche, he drew up an agreement with master Nicolas from Beaumont-le-Roger. There he indicated very specifically that the architect was to model his design on the tower of Nogent and produce a structure 115 feet high and 82 feet in diameter. The contract price was to be 1175 *livres parisis* (livres of Paris), the patron providing stone, sand, lime, and water. The architect was completely responsible for the project, since he had to pay the workers.

Rivalry

The patron did not hesitate to make architects compete with one another. The case of Canterbury Cathedral, devastated by a fire in 1174, illustrates this point admirably. Faced with such a terrible disaster, the monks called in several architects, some English, others from France, and obtained detailed reports before deciding who to appoint. Their choice fell on William of Sens (from Normandy), who had impressed them with his analysis of the work that needed to be undertaken, clearly distinguishing the parts that had to be destroyed completely and those that could safely be preserved. Once appointed, he immediately began work, but a crippling fall forced

Gothic architecture began in France, in the area around Paris. In England its appearance was due to the choice of a French architect, William of Sens, for the construction of Canterbury Cathedral. Nothing is known of him before his arrival in England, but he must have had ample experience to win over the monks. Left: Canterbury's much later (15th-century) crossing tower, and (above) Trinity Chapel, completed by William's successor, William the Englishman.

him to take to his bed and eventually return to his homeland. His successor, William the Englishman, carried on with the work, respecting the initial design, which had marked the acceptance by the monks of the new style from France.

This is how the first fully Gothic building on English soil came to be constructed. For some time its influence was sporadic, and England long retained a fondness for certain Romanesque features.

Specialized Architects

Specialized groups of architects came into being. The arrangement lasted only for a generation, however, since it was closely involved with political events—the fight to the death waged by Capetians and Plantagenets for the control of France. In this field, as in many others, the latter held the upper hand. Henry II of England (1154–89), a Plantagenet, decided to build fortresses in order to secure his vulnerable new territories. The records of crown revenue and expenditure mention *ingeniatores* (engineers). Some of them appear to be English, like Alnoth, while the majority were French—Roger Engonet, Richard, Maurice the Mason, Raoul de Gramont. The castles of Dover, Gisors, and many new constructions were their work.

The Capetian king Philip Augustus continued this policy and greatly extended it. Between 1189 and 1206, sixteen architects with specific skills laid the defenses of the

English military architects conceived of huge self-contained complexes composed of a series of concentric walls and buildings designed to protect each other. In France, on the other hand, the architects under Philip Augustus preferred strong, easily defended castles that were closely linked to towns. Round towers, found in scores of towns, stood as symbols of Capetian power.

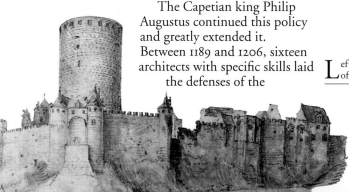

Left: The Great Tower of Bourges.

kingdom by building fortresses linked to recaptured cities. The king even created a council, over which he presided, to advise him on how best to act quickly and at the lowest possible cost. In Paris, the city walls protecting the right bank, strengthened on the west by the tower of the Louvre, were erected in 1190; they included twenty circular towers built to the same design, 102 feet high and 49 feet wide. Many towns were surrounded by fortifications on the Parisian model, with well-built walls, regularly spaced towers,

Dover is a distinctively English fortress. The same type is also to be found in France in Plantagenet King Richard the Lionheart's Château Gaillard in Normandy.

and a limited number of entrances. Each of the architects recruited for this huge operation had his own specialty: Some constructed moats; eleven of them, referred to in documents as *magistri* (masters), had overall responsibility.

The Status of the Major 13th-Century Architects

A radical change occurred at the beginning of the 13th century: The architect could no longer assume all the responsibility. The administrative authorities had to create a financial division to deal instantly with demands that might arise on the building site, to

The west rose window of Reims (above) is set in a larger glass area, allowing even more light to flood in. The openwork gable below it (opposite) is no less daring, set with statues of the Coronation of the Virgin.

maintain supplies, and to pay the workers regularly. Freed from these tasks, the architect acquired a new status, outside the hierarchy of medieval society.

It is obvious from texts and illustrations of the period that this privileged, powerful position annoyed many people. In a famous sermon of 1261, Nicolas de Biard recorded his irritation: "In these huge buildings there is an architect who directs by word alone and who seldom or never dirties his hands; however, he receives a much larger recompense than the others. Architects with sticks and gloves in hand say to the others: 'Cut me this stone here.' They do no work yet they receive much greater reward." This kind of criticism has been leveled in all ages at those whose genius permits them to enjoy positions of command and financial ease.

Rayonnant Architecture

The remarkable new position of the architect is connected with a new period in Gothic architecture, launched in 1231 with the proposed

Architects of the 13th century fascinated their contemporaries, who saw so many wonderful monuments rising around them. It is easy to understand why they were often represented on tombstones drawing complicated designs, as on this anonymous mid-13th-century slab in St.-Ouen at Rouen.

The daring of 13th-century architects reached a peak in the Ste.-Chapelle in Paris, consecrated in 1248. The architect, who is still unknown, but may have been Jean de Chelles or Pierre de Montreuil, created a structure that broke all the rules. The patron—the king—wanted to house the most precious relics of Christendom, those of Christ's Passion, in a chapel that would be both a palace and a shrine. The architect conceived the building as a reliquary, enclosed within more than seven hundred square yards of stained glass. The west rose window (left) was put in place in the last decade of the 15th century, under Charles VIII, and is in a style very different from that of the 13th century, though it boasts equally magical colors.

resumption of work on the abbey church of St.-Denis. This style has been given the evocative name of "Rayonnant" (radiant), because of the radiating pattern of the rose windows that became almost compulsory in ecclesiastical buildings. To contemporaries it was known as *opus francigenum* (the work of the French), recalling its origin, and it spread at once through Western Europe: In the Holy Roman Empire there was the nave of Strasbourg, in England Westminster Abbey, in Italy the church of S. Francesco at Assisi, in Sweden Uppsala Cathedral, and, far overseas, in Cyprus, Famagusta Cathedral.

The abbot of St.-Ouen in Rouen, Jean Roussel, laid the first stone of a new abbey church (above) in 1318, dreaming, as so many others did, of building the Heavenly Jerusalem on earth. Work went on over two centuries, involving generations of architects.

It is understandable that contemporaries, struck by this architectural style that made empty space triumph over solid masonry and so flooded the building with light, should have remembered the names of these creative magicians. Some—Jean de Chelles, Pierre de Montreuil, Robert de Coucy, Peter Parler, Henry Yevele, and many others—have become as famous as the great heroes of history.

Tributes in Stone: Signatures and Tomb Slabs

In Notre-Dame in Paris, at the request of the bishop, Pierre de Montreuil inscribed in beautiful Gothic lettering the name of his predecessor, Jean de Chelles, who had laid the first stone of the south transept on 11 February 1258. In the late 13th century the practice arose of inscribing architects' names in the stone labyrinth patterns on the nave floor. The labyrinths were installed some time after the facts they record—the one at Reims dates from the end of the century, that at Amiens from 1288—which explains occasional errors and omissions. Care was taken at Amiens to make clear the order of succession, from Robert de Luzarches to Thomas de Cormont to Cormont's son Renaud, and to include a depiction of the patron, Bishop Evrard de Fouilloy. At Reims, archbishop Aubry de Humbert appeared in the center, surrounded by the master masons Jean d'Orbais, Jean le Loup, Gaucher de Reims, and Bernard de Soissons. Architects were also given titles reflecting not so much their technical mastery as their intellectual worth. Pierre de Montreuil, to whom the monks of St.-Germain-des-Prés wished to pay exceptional tribute, is entombed with his wife at his side in the Lady Chapel, which he had built, and honored with the university title of *doctor lathomorum*, or "doctor of stones."

Opposite left: The tombstone of two architects, father and son, who worked at St.-Ouen in the 15th century. It was put up by Colin, the son, and its inscription mentions only the father: "Here lies Master Alexandre de Berneval, master of the works and Masonry of our lord the king in the bailiwick of Rouen and of this church, who died in the year of grace MCDXC [1490], the V day of January. Pray for his soul."

The labyrinth pattern on the floor of Reims Cathedral links patron and architects.

Tombs of esteemed architects were frequently placed inside churches. Tomb slabs recall the most famous of them, though some have been worn illegible by the feet of the faithful. Examples are Hugues Libergier at St.-Nicaise in Reims and Alexandre and Colin de Berneval at St.-Ouen in Rouen. Their social status is shown in the way they are dressed like great lords, and identified by the tools of their trade, such as compass and rod, or a model of their building.

Images on Parchment

Architects are also recorded in a number of manuscripts

that tell us about the building process, concentrating on their role and their close relationship with the patron. It was the patron who gave the orders, which were then transmitted to the workers.

Examination of these records provides evidence of the dialectical nature of the relationship between patron and architect, just as the latter was acquiring greater importance.

The example of Prague is revealing. The future Emperor Charles IV, having decided to endow the capital of Bohemia with a cathedral as large as his political ambition, gave the commission to a French architect, Matthew of Arras. Matthew was active from 1344 to 1352, but then suffered an accident on the building site. In 1354 he was replaced by another architect, the German Peter Parler, who completely reformulated his predecessor's project with a German concept. Charles IV included depictions of both in the building.

Associates of Princes

In France at the same period relationships were very different, as architects became more like members of

the patron's family. Raymond du Temple, who had built the Grande Vis—the great spiral staircase in the Louvre —became an intimate of the king. Charles V was godfather to Raymond's son Charlot and in 1376 gave him 220 gold florins "in recognizance of all the good and pleasant services which our friend, sergeant, and mason, Raymond du Temple, has done and is still doing for us daily and which we hope he will continue to do in the future, and in order to maintain and keep our godson in studies at Orléans, where he is at present a scholar, and to buy him books and other necessities." This close association between creative artist and patron is found throughout the

The cathedral of St. Vitus in Prague (opposite right) is a characteristic example of the medieval approach to building. For Emperor Charles IV (above), it was a matter of creating a work that was significant at three levels— politically, for Prague was the capital of the empire; feudally, for the cathedral was situated in the palace of the dukes of Bohemia; and artistically, a determination that led him to call on a French architect, Matthew of Arras (opposite left). Matthew's death, political developments, and the changing ideas of style caused the emperor to turn to a new architect, Peter Parler (left). Unity was preserved, however, in the technique used and was evoked by placing busts of the two architects and the patron in the choir triforium.

second half of the 14th century and at the beginning of the 15th in princely courts including Dijon, Bourges, London, and Milan.

The Architect's Independence

The accepted, established role of the architect was to have disturbing repercussions for the patron. The most famous architects might be less than punctilious on site, and because they might often be involved with many projects, they were often not present. Contracts offered attractive financial rewards but also heavy constraints for absenteeism.

The earliest known contract is the one between the clergy of Meaux and the architect Gautier de Varinfroy, who was to earn ten livres a year for the duration of the work and ten sous a day when present. In return, he undertook not to accept commissions outside the diocese without express permission; not to leave Meaux for more than two months and not to go to the building site at Evreux that he directed or any other construction site in the diocese without the chapter's permission; and finally, he was to stay in Meaux.

The 1261 contract between the abbot of St.-Gilles du Gard and the architect Martin de Lonay, who lived nearby at Pasquières, is no less stringent: He was to earn two *sous tournois* (sous of Tours) a day on the condition that he worked before midday; his meal expenses were the subject of particularly lengthy negotiations; and he would receive an additional 100 sous tournois on Whitsunday for clothing. In return, he was to reside at St.-Gilles from Michaelmas to

The Butter Tower of Rouen Cathedral provoked a dispute between the canons and the architect. A council of masters called to settle the conflict produced no resolution. Jacques le Roux finally resigned on 27 January 1508 and was replaced by his nephew, Rolland le Roux. In the end a tower without a spire was built, in accordance with the client's wishes.

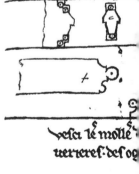

Whitsunday. He was not banned from working elsewhere, but he had little opportunity to do so. When Jacques Favran was hired at Gerona in 1312, the contract stated the amount to be paid—1000 sous of Barcelona, on the condition that he went there every two months—but no longer mentioned any ban on directing work at other sites.

Artists' Rights

Distrust became more and more marked between architects and patrons. At Toul in 1381, the chapter insisted that Pierre Perrat renounce ownership of the wooden templates used to determine the molding profiles of stones. This

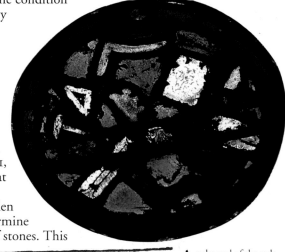

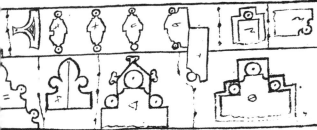

was the first time that the delicate question of artistic ownership had been raised, and the matter was resolved in the patron's favor. Later, by covenant of 9 May 1460, the architect Hattonchâtel surrendered the drawing for the facade of Toul Cathedral, leaving the chapter in total control over its execution.

At the end of the 15th century, the relationship between the partners was no longer the same, as the balance established in the 13th century was disturbed by some over-strong personalities. The value of technical skill had been proclaimed in stained-glass windows, as at Chartres (above), and in drawings by Villard de Honnecourt (left). However, the role of stonecutters was reduced and eventually disappeared completely, leaving a vast gulf between the patron and the architects.

"If a master mason has agreed to build a work and has made a drawing of the work as it is to be executed, he must not change this original design. But he must carry out the work according to the plan that he has presented to the lords, towns, or villages in such a way that the work will not be diminished or lessened in value."

Statute of the Strasbourg stonecutters, article 10, 1459

CHAPTER III
MEANS OF EXPRESSION

Opposite: Detail of a large drawing for the west front of Strasbourg Cathedral, c. 1360–5. Right: An architect's assistant using dividers.

The architect's responsibilities—to provide the design and manage the project—required special skills. In the matter of the design, architects had to persuade the patron and avoid any temperamental clashes that might lead to changes of mind and introduce inconsistencies. On site, it was vital for them to make themselves understood by the different people who had to work together, to prevent the scheme from going wrong. When building in stone, architects had to produce two kinds of documents: One would enable the patron to visualize the final result, and the other would guide the different various workers. Later, we find another kind of drawing—sketches that show the architect working toward the final design through various changes of mind; it is probable that such sketches also existed in the Middle Ages, even though we have no written evidence and not one has been preserved.

No detailed designs at all are known before the 13th century. From that it has been assumed that the medieval architect was happy to communicate in speech, correcting or modifying the original design as the building went along. Yet this assumption ignores the technical mastery that is evident in the great monuments of the Middle Ages.

Models have often been used as a means of communication between the architect and the patron. The wooden model of the pilgrimage church Zur Schönen Maria at Regensburg (right) was made c. 1520, according to a design by Hieber. It is of exceptional quality.

The model of St.-Maclou at Rouen (above), made after 1521, gives a faithful and complete image of the building. It is made of wood and papier-mâché and stands more than three feet tall.

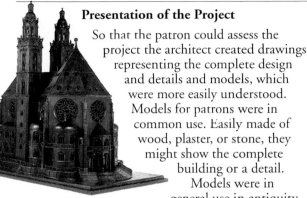

Presentation of the Project

So that the patron could assess the project the architect created drawings representing the complete design and details and models, which were more easily understood. Models for patrons were in common use. Easily made of wood, plaster, or stone, they might show the complete building or a detail. Models were in general use in antiquity but seemed to have disappeared between the Carolingian era and the beginning of the 16th century in northern Europe. However, there is some evidence of them in Italy in the 14th century and in France in the 15th. In the process of building the abbey of St.-Médard at Soissons, a wax model was made.

On tombs, the founders of religious buildings are often shown holding a small model of the edifice. The oldest

The existence of models before the 16th century is confirmed by the presence of small ones held in the founder's hand on tomb effigies. This one, of a mid-13th-century Count Palatine, is preserved at Nuremberg.

example, which dates from the middle of the 12th century, is the recumbent figure of King Childebert, founder of the basilica of St.-Vincent-Ste.-Croix in Paris. From the beginning of the 14th century, the founder may appear on the portal of the church presenting a model of the building, as with the figure of Enguerrand de Marigny on the collegiate church of Ecouis.

Surviving Architectural Drawings

Drawings were no doubt more expensive because of the high cost of parchment. The oldest to survive come from the Oeuvre Notre-Dame at Strasbourg, the body responsible for building work, composed of the fabric committee of the cathedral and the masons' lodge. One of them dates back to the years 1250–60 and shows us the first design for the west facade planned to complete the nave, itself probably conceived by an architect trained in Paris. The other drawings show changes to this first design, which in the end was not carried out.

Throughout this period, other workshops were equally conscientious in preserving architectural drawings, for instance at Ulm, Vienna, Freiburg-im-Breisgau, and Clermont-Ferrand. These show not only facades but also side elevations

The model of the Rieux chapel, which was added to the chevet of the Franciscan church in Toulouse between 1333 and 1344, is held by its founder Jean Tissandier. Here the representation is clearly not symbolic, but very specific. Such small-scale models became more and more precise.

(Cologne), sections (Prague), and chapels (Strasbourg). There is no doubt about their purpose: The 1381 agreement for the rebuilding of the belltower of La Daurade at Toulouse involved a "little roll of parchment." Better still, the contract for the cloister portal of the Hôpital St.-Jacques in Paris, dated 1474, came with an architectural drawing that survives today. It was the work of Guillaume Monnin, stonecutter, and was intended for the hospital governors, to let them judge the final appearance of the work.

How Architectural Drawings Reached the Workshop

The drawings submitted to the patron were not detailed enough for the execution of the building. The architect had to produce other drawings to make his ideas clear to the workshop. These generally disappeared during the course of the works, but a few are still in existence, such as a drawing at Strasbourg showing the re-vaulting of Ste.-Catherine's chapel, begun by Bernhard Nonnenmacher in 1542. It bears numbers and letters indicating precisely how to cut the stones for

The idea of constructing a belfry between the two tower stumps at Strasbourg Cathedral dates from the years 1360–5. It was given a great deal of thought, reflected in the largest surviving medieval architectural drawing, 13.5 feet high (left). It also gives a precise indication in color of the sculptural program (see pages 1–9).

The seal of the Oeuvre Notre-Dame of Strasbourg of 1486 (above), responsible for the construction projects of the church, depicts the facade of the cathedral and emphasizes the belfry.

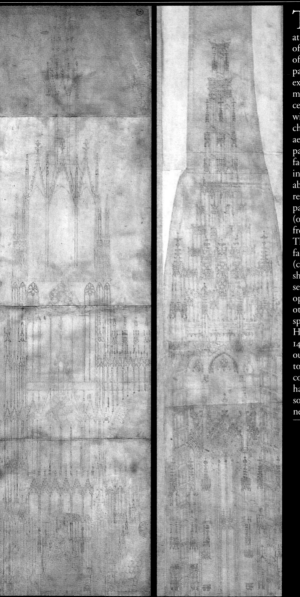

The museum of the Oeuvre Notre-Dame at Strasbourg contains one of the richest collections of drawings on parchment. The oldest examples go back to the middle of the 13th century. They bear witness to the patrons' changes of mind in aesthetic matters, particularly over the facade, but they also include designs abandoned for technical reasons. The drawing for part of the facade (opposite) is a project from around 1250–60. The elevation of half the facade with a spire (center), dated 1275, shows for the first time a series of arcades and openings one above the other. The elevation of the spire (left), drawn by Hans Hammer before 1490, follows the broad outlines of the north tower, which was completed in 1439. It may have been a plan for the south tower, which was never built.

the vaulting ribs. In another drawing for the west buttress of Strasbourg Cathedral (datable to c. 1350–65), the design is shown at three levels—ground, rose window, and belfry—superimposed one on the other. Many other drawings exist that are very difficult to understand.

Working Drawings

There are some examples, mostly in France, of what have been called tracings, that is painted architectural drawings incised in stone, to a depth of 2–3 millimeters, showing an architectural detail to scale. The oldest example recorded, at the Cistercian abbey of Byland (North

It was customary to produce full-size working drawings, in order to guide the stonecutters. Some of them, incised in stone, have been miraculously preserved. On the east wall of the triforium in the south transept of Reims Cathedral, there is a drawing of the inner side of the central west portal as executed. There is a similar drawing of the flanking portal on the west wall (left above). Though they are sketchy they are very precise—drawn to scale and showing both elevation and ground plan.

The same system is used in the 20th century when restoration work is being done. This drawing (left) for the spire or conical roof over the spiral staircase of the Hôtel de Cluny in Paris shows both elevation and plan, showing the different courses; markings in color indicate stones to be replaced.

Yorkshire), dates from the end of the 12th century. This first tracing illustrates a west rose window, while the second shows the central part of the same window. The precise, geometric cutting of stone was no longer the concern of the architect but of a specialist, referred to in texts as a dresser of stone.

Working drawings were usually made on perishable material in "tracing houses" (i.e., drawing offices) —first mentioned in 1324—and disappeared when the workshop was disbanded. Drawings incised directly into stone—probably never a widespread practice—have been found on the floor (for instance in the axial chapel of Narbonne Cathedral), on the

In the sacristy of the Roslin chapel in Scotland, where construction began in 1450, the north and south walls contain incised drawings from which the templates for the different ribs and pinnacles would have been made. They appear strangely superimposed, but they would have been clear to those who used them.

exterior walls of the choir (at Clermont-Ferrand), and on the walls of the transept (at Reims). In these examples the drawings are full-size. Others are on a reduced scale. In the south transept of Soissons, there are small-scale schematic drawings of two rose windows; one is perhaps that of the west facade of Chartres, the other that of the north transept of Laon. Other examples of small-scale drawings, serving as memoranda for the architect, occur at the hospital of St. John the Evangelist in Cambridge, the Benedictine church of Gegenbach, and Leighton Buzzard church.

Templates: The Workshop's Memory

Manuscripts fairly often mention the existence of templates, and they are sometimes illustrated. They are simple units, generally cut out of wood, which give the profile of a base, a rib, or any molding. The earliest depictions, dating from the beginning of the 13th century, occur at Chartres where, in the stained-glass window of St. Chéron, several templates are shown in the sculptors' lodge, carefully hung up. We see them again in the medallion recording stone-cutters' tools.

A little later, Villard de Honnecourt's sketchbook gives particularly valuable information about them. Knowing their importance, Villard drew the different templates used in the construction

For an architect anxious to maintain control over a project, it was essential to be able to make drawings. A place was put at his disposal, which is sometimes mentioned in documents as a *trasura*—"tracing house" or drawing office. Such rooms existed at Rouen, Strasbourg, and Paris, and some survive in England, in particular at Wells and at York (opposite).

Tracings were not used only for work in stone. Carpenters today still use the same technique.

of the radiating chapels of Reims Cathedral, for mullions, vaulting ribs, transverse arches, and wall arches. He even indicated by a distinctive sign the direction in which they were to be placed in relation to the grain of the stone. While drawings survive at Strasbourg, Ulm, and Vienna, we have nothing at all for

other major buildings, and there too Villard de Honnecourt's sketchbook gives important information, particularly concerning work at Reims.

At York a tracing house was specially fitted out by the masons with a fireplace and a closet where the templates are still kept. The tracing floor, 23 x 13 feet, entirely free of posts or columns, was intended to receive full-size drawings, created, as they had to be, by very simple instruments: set square and dividers. On this floor there are still incised drawings (below) that have been identified with the tracery in the side aisles of the minster chancel (c. 1360).

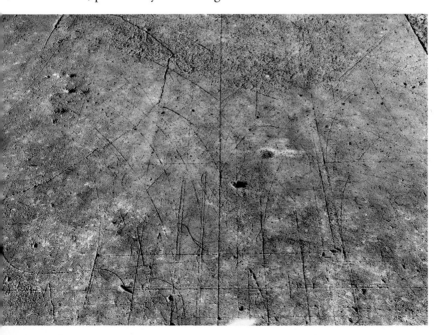

The quality of a building and its construction relied on consistency. The long time it took to create each of the architectural elements could easily lead to accidental variations. Thus it was necessary to keep a record of such things as molding profiles in the form of templates. A stained-glass window at Chartres (left) of the early 13th century shows two wooden templates —colored yellow— hanging below dividers in the stonecutters' workshop.

Villard de Honnecourt

A remarkable collection of drawings, begun by Villard around the 1220s, has been known since the middle of the 19th century. In it he states his aims: "In this book you will find advice on building in stone, on machines used in carpentry, on the art of portraiture, on drawing, and on the art of geometry." He never calls himself an architect, and interpretations that assume that he was one only serve to obscure the true man. He was, above all, an inquisitive person, curious about everything, especially about the technological advances made in his time. In order to satisfy his unending curiosity, he found material where he could, not always at first hand. (This accounts for the many errors that have recently been pointed out.)

When he says that he had drawn a lion "from nature," he may have been able to fool his contemporaries, but now it is obvious that he must have been closely copying another illustration; similarly his so-called tomb of a Saracen turns out to be one wing of an antique diptych. He reproduces machines, such as a hydraulic saw, whose mechanism was not always clear to him.

These few reservations do not in any way detract from Villard's genius, which was exceptional for his time, nor do they lessen the light he sheds on it. All but one of his architectural drawings relate to existing buildings, but the differences are too great for them to have been intended as straightforward depictions of the actual structure. The drawings of the rose windows at Lausanne and Chartres are so unlike the present

Villard de Honnecourt drew templates, in particular those used in the construction of the eastern chapel of Reims Cathedral (above). He was equally interested in the latest mechanical developments, such as a hydraulic saw (below).

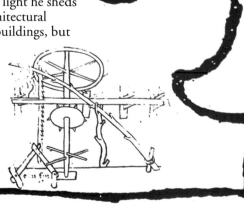

windows that it cannot be a case of bad drafts-manship. The same is true, as all the critics have pointed out, of the exterior and interior elevations and sections of Reims. In these cases, we have to assume that Villard reproduced images that he had been given.

Inscriptions on some of Villard's drawings point in the same direction. Some features had already been built, he notes (the radiating chapels), while

Villard de Honnecourt stayed in Reims for a long time. There he studied drawings of French and Swiss buildings assembled by the architect in charge as a sort of design archive. Villard copied some of them without worrying whether they corresponded to reality. The oxen, not the architectural forms, interested him most in the tower of Laon Cathedral (left and page 106).

some had still to be built (for instance one of the crossing piers). It seems likely that the architect of Reims had given him a collection of drawings, including abandoned schemes which, for some reason or another, particularly intrigued Villard. He also provided him with templates used for the construction of the radiating chapels. One even wonders whether the

architect of Reims might have shown Villard drawings of other buildings used to stimulate his imagination before embarking on such a major project. The fact that Villard shows only details, and not complete buildings, lends weight to this theory. In that case, what we have would be eloquent testimony about the conception of a major project, starting with images of existing structures elsewhere to serve as sources.

Left: Villard de Honnecourt's drawing of the rose window at Lausanne. Above: The window as actually built. His drawing must have been based on a rejected design.

For Reims Cathedral, Villard did not try to record the section and elevation of the finished building, but he copied a project that he no doubt knew had been abandoned for reasons now unknown. He seems to have simplified his various drawings so as to retain only certain points: flying buttresses in double flights and double tiers (left), window tracery which he made more legible by leaving out the flying buttresses (opposite right). Comparison with an accurate modern drawing (opposite left) brings out the similarities and differences.

Drawings constituted the living memory of the workshop, and they were indispensable for the patron who wanted to avoid changes in the original design. They were necessary in cases such as Reims Cathedral, a model of consistency, which was started in 1211—but its facade was not begun until fifty years later. And as today, the patron could not be expected to make a decision without seeing the design in visual form, whether drawing or model.

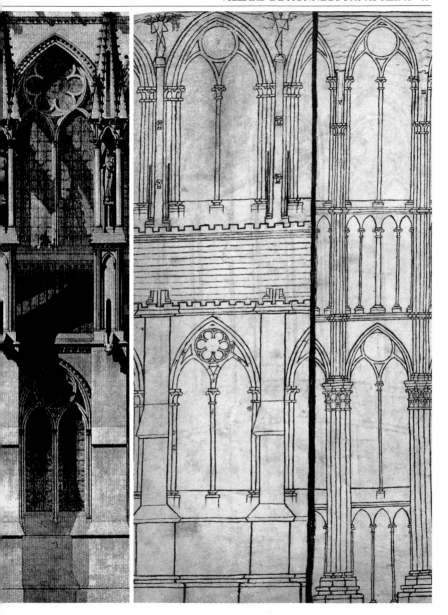

"We hereby make known that Etienne de Bonneuil, stonecutter, came before us undertaking as master mason to build the church of Uppsala in Sweden, who proposed going into that land, according to his words. And it is recognized in law that he shall lead and take, at the cost of the said church, together with him, ten journeymen and ten apprentices as he sees that it shall be to the efficiency and profit of the said church."

Act passed before the Provost of Paris
30 August 1287

CHAPTER IV
ON SITE

By the end of the 15th century the era of great cathedral building was finished, but artists were fascinated by Gothic grandeur. Opposite: A miniature by Jean Colombe of the reconstruction of Troy. Right: A mason depicted on one of the bosses of Norwich Cathedral cloister.

It is difficult to generalize about the organization
of the building site. It varied depending on the date
(progress was usually enormous, but there were also
times of regression), the region, the financial resources
available, and finally the people involved, whose
talent and technical knowledge were not uniform.

Europe of the Builders

In stone building the extraordinary progress of
northern regions of France—Normandy in the 11th
century and the Ile-de-France (the area around Paris)
in the 12th and 13th centuries—cannot be denied. In
other regions the appearance of a new style, generally
linked to a different technique, follows the arrival
of teams of foreigners in the area.
To achieve a revolution in art, it
is not enough to find a
great architect; there also
have to be high caliber
workers.

Gothic building
techniques spread
through highly skilled
French architects and
technicians called to
distant building sites.
They were solemnly
received in Rhodes in
1480 (below). The
carpenters come first,
before the masons; on
the ground are a mortar-
trough, dividers, set
square, mallet, and rasp.

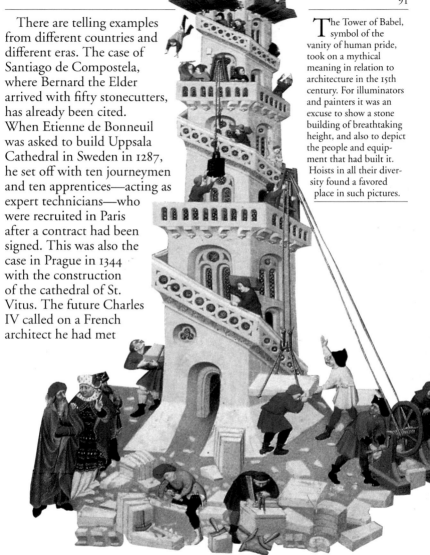

There are telling examples from different countries and different eras. The case of Santiago de Compostela, where Bernard the Elder arrived with fifty stonecutters, has already been cited. When Etienne de Bonneuil was asked to build Uppsala Cathedral in Sweden in 1287, he set off with ten journeymen and ten apprentices—acting as expert technicians—who were recruited in Paris after a contract had been signed. This was also the case in Prague in 1344 with the construction of the cathedral of St. Vitus. The future Charles IV called on a French architect he had met

The Tower of Babel, symbol of the vanity of human pride, took on a mythical meaning in relation to architecture in the 15th century. For illuminators and painters it was an excuse to show a stone building of breathtaking height, and also to depict the people and equipment that had built it. Hoists in all their diversity found a favored place in such pictures.

at Avignon, Matthew of Arras, and persuaded him to build a French-style cathedral. Matthew set out with a team of technicians he knew he could not find in Bohemia, notably stone dressers and -cutters.

The choice of those architects brought a heavy additional cost, which often tested the patron's ambition. But it was not always so: William of Sens found men who were capable of fulfilling his demands on the spot when he went to Canterbury, for the English had been trained in building in stone since the time of William the Conqueror.

Organized Guilds

Then as now, building in stone brought together on site two major craft guilds, the carpenters and the masons. (There are many others whose function is more limited and therefore more difficult to situate. Metalwork, for example, was to play an increasingly important role, but its organization into guilds has not yet been analyzed.) As time went on, progress took

In the 11th century carpenters began to yield to masons and confine themselves to the building of complicated timber roofs, which were destined to be concealed by stone vaults. Many have been destroyed by fire, but some remarkable ones survive in England. The greatest feat was the construction of a spire, which required

lengthy calculations and assembly on the ground before it could be set in place; the one for Salisbury Cathedral (left) is one of the most spectacular. Above: A corbel in Gloucester Cathedral showing master and apprentice.

the form of great technical advances, though there were some setbacks. In northern Europe the results were spectacular, and while there were greater developments in masonry construction, we find such outstanding timber structures as the octagon set over the crossing of Ely Cathedral after 1322 by William Hurley. The most stunning examples of work in stone are also to be found in northern Europe during the 14th century.

German, English, and French architects showed their greatest audacity in vaulting. The English invention of the fan vault led to the achievement of King's College Chapel at Cambridge, begun in 1446

For the octagon of Ely Cathedral in 1322, the carpenter William Hurley tried to create the illusion of stone in wood by pretending that his two-tier design was a rib vault. The lightness of the material allowed him to cover a vast space and light it with a continuous row of high windows.

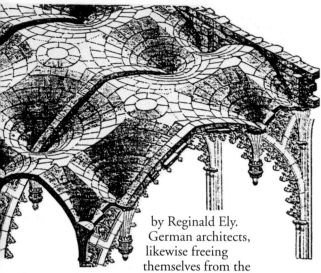

At the end of the 15th century, command of stereotomy (the precise, geometrical cutting of stone) produced some remarkable achievements in most European countries. English architects created the fan vault. Its technical nature disappeared under decoration that looked like a structural rib system but was in fact incised into the blocks of stone, as in King's College Chapel at Cambridge (opposite). The sketch of the upper side of the vault of Henry VII's Chapel at Westminster Abbey (left), built a little later, in 1502, shows the highest achievement of fan vaulting. As before, it begins with half-cones along the walls, but the vault is almost flat, resting on arches that also support two rows of full cones that terminate in pendants.

by Reginald Ely. German architects, likewise freeing themselves from the over-rigid formula of the quadripartite vault, succeeded in vaulting the Vladislav Hall of Prague Castle with a single span 52 feet wide and 43 feet high covered with freely curving ribs. French architects, though less audacious, completely overcame all the problems of the weight of the vaulting in such buildings as St.-Nicolas-de-Port, near Nancy, begun in 1481.

Building Manuals

This technical mastery was the result of increased professionalism and specialization. It is not easy to reconstruct the process by which this came about, but one can make some headway by studying various documents, especially personal accounts. In the lands of the Holy Roman Empire, the late 15th century saw the appearance of works on building techniques, which became the construction manuals of the Renaissance. In France, 16th-century architect Philibert Delorme retained something of medieval thought and techniques in what he wrote. The earliest technical treatise is that by Matthäus Roritzer, master

mason of Regensburg Cathedral
(1486). Many of these works
were limited in scope, illustrating
"recipes" for details that could
only be understood by other
professionals. In any case, it is impossible to
know whether they circulated beyond a very
restricted circle.

Different Men, Specialized Crafts

On site the gap grew between the intellectuals
and the minor craftsmen, who outnumbered
them by far. Carriers of water, stone, and lime
are often represented in illuminated manuscripts; they were paid by the piece, or better
still by the day, and recruited locally. A
significant step higher up the scale were
the men who mixed the mortar. Their task
was one that
demanded
great

Manuals were
created as
technical advances were
made from the 13th

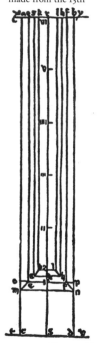

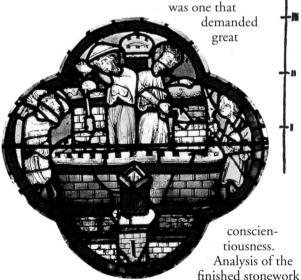

conscien-
tiousness.
Analysis of the
finished stonework
shows subtle variations, generally due to differences
in training. It is clear from the accounts that pay
varied according to training and the skills

century—illustrated by a
stained-glass window at
Bourges (left)—to the
15th century. Matthäus
Roritzer's manual shows
the importance of
geometry. He establishes
the elevation from a plan
made with the help of
a compass and a ruler,
achieving "just
proportions."

involved in the work. Financial comparisons, however, are not easy since gross pay did not exist and wages were topped off by what we would today call payment in kind.

Skilled Trades

The masons, who laid the stones for the walls, seem, according to some accounts, to have belonged to a higher rank. The variations, which are not always easy to understand, can be explained by different practices from one site to another.

Stonecutters had an especially important role: They were the essential link between the architect or the warden transmitting the architect's instructions and the actual construction process. They had a decisive effect upon technical development. It was to their credit that the transition had been made from rustic architecture, in which stone was shaped with hammers, to building with dressed stone, with small vertical and horizontal joints. This revolution took place at the beginning of the 11th century in certain exceptional workshops. Chroniclers, who until then had been used to crude buildings, were impressed

In this 15th-century illustration of the building of the Tower of Babel, the architect looks like a wizard.

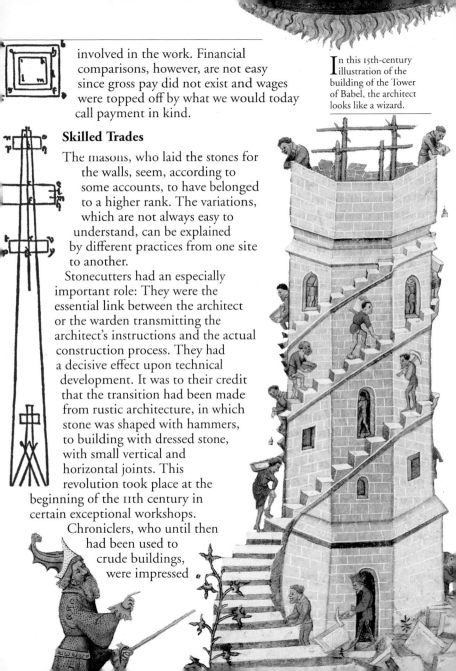

enough by the
new ones to
express their
wonder. Later
in the century,
they became
accustomed to
the sight and had
less to say. Three
elements were
necessary to achieve
such success: The
stonecutter had to
be well trained, he
had to have well-
made tools, and
the building
material had to
be of high
quality. Written
documents, which
are generally not
very explicit,
provide little
information on
these points; the
monuments
themselves are
more instructive,
and vary
remarkably.

Signatures in Stone

Masons' marks are
a valuable source
of information.
Elegantly incised
on the visible face of the stone,
these autographs are evidence of
the pride the man who cut them

took in his work. The same marks appear in a number of different buildings, giving us chronological pointers.

The church of St.-Germain-des-Prés in Paris provides revealing evidence. Abbot Morard had begun its reconstruction with a bell-tower porch, which was finished at the time of his death (1014). Work continued with the construction of the chapel of St. Symphorien to the south, then with the bell towers, to the east of the transept, and finally with the nave. The stones are covered with masons' marks, some of which occur throughout the different sections, leading to the conclusion that all these parts were built by a single generation of workers.

At Tewkesbury, England, masons' marks occur that are identical to ones seen in France; the stonecutters had clearly crossed the Channel from one building site to the other. Once the wall was built, they allowed the stonecutter to be paid by the piece, while also allowing the quality of the cutting to be judged. The marks' disappearance was linked to the beginning of another form of payment, either by the volume of work done at the bench or, when the chosen technique did not need such detailed attention, by the day. The custom of masons' marks also varied depending on the region

From the beginning of the 11th century, Parisian stonecutters put their personal marks on cornerstones. This example (above), shaped like a key, is on the porch of the church of St.-Germain-des-Prés. Opposite: Medieval architects and masons were masters of the technique of replacing the supports in a building while leaving the upper parts undisturbed. In 1231, for instance, the architect of the new choir of St.-Denis retained the early ambulatory vaults, and when he replaced the main arcade piers, he kept the original 12th-century abaci on which the vaults rested. An early-16th-century illumination shows one way of carrying out this delicate operation (left).

and the institution. It is also possible that building projects structured on capitalist lines may have existed just as we know them today. There is no documentary evidence for this theory, but it is worth considering, especially in the case of cities, where there was intense building activity, as in Paris from the 11th century on. From the middle of the 12th century, the pace of development grew quicker and never slowed down.

The Cistercian "Mercenaries"

Cistercian architecture sheds interesting light on this point. The difficulties encountered by the order in the management of the lay brothers are well known; at the end of the 12th century, the lay

Medieval representations of building sites depict every craft—from cutting stone to setting it in its place—at the same time. Images of the Tower of Babel (above) exemplify all this human activity, added to which are mechanical contraptions like the double block crane, here worked by a windlass.

brothers revolted, refusing to perform the tasks imposed on them. In the middle of the 13th century, far fewer men entered the monasteries, leading to the employment of outsiders who had to be paid. As early as 1133 St. Bernard had begun to hire workers to help the monks erect new buildings at Clairvaux. The Rule of the Order even alluded to people then called "mercenaries." They were paid by the piece and left traces of their passage by signing ashlar blocks at Flaran, Sénanque, and many other abbeys. The beauty of the incised marks strikingly matches the quality of the work; the Cistercians had made it a point of honor to recruit the best stonecutters.

Building Firms

It seems that these individual marks became those of the master. Five workshops were set up in Paris in 1500 to carry out the construction of the Notre-Dame bridge. At the head of each one there was a master mason—stonecutter, with fourteen masons

A 15th-century sculptor represented Cistercians as builders. Left: St. Bernard holding a model in his hand to emphasize his role in establishing and building abbeys. An illustration from the second half of the 16th century (below) depicts the construction of the Cistercian abbey of Schönau, near Heidelberg in Germany, and is remarkable in showing monks laboring alongside other workers.

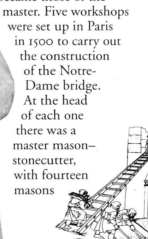

under him who inscribed the dressed stones with the master's mark.

Beaumaris Castle in Wales is one building project among many, but is more straightforward to analyze than the others. Doing so helps in understanding the organization of manpower. Beaumaris is admittedly a royal building site. The accounts for 1268–70 indicate the presence of 1630 workmen, 400 masons, 30 blacksmiths or carpenters, and 1000 unskilled laborers and carters. Numbers of this order are generally a sign of a well-supplied building site with no financial constraints. The fabric accounts of St. Lazare at Autun in France for the period 1294–5 give a few details of pay: Unskilled laborers received 7 deniers, the plasterers and men who made the mortar 10 or 11 deniers, and masons and

stonecutters received 20 to 22 deniers. Between the top and bottom of the ladder, the ratio is three to one, underlining once again the strong hierarchical divisions of the time.

The Prime Material: Stone

Building quality depends on the careful choice of materials. In the Middle Ages, just as in antiquity, people found themselves confronted by this difficult problem, which our age sadly knows only too well. When we undertake the restoration of old buildings we often find that the original quarries are exhausted or can no longer supply such good stone.

In the 11th century, when a widespread upsurge of building took place on a huge scale,

Among the architect's concerns were the transport and handling of stone on the building site. A photograph of the crossing of Reims Cathedral after shelling in 1917 shows the different types of material used in the work: dressed stone, stone carved with moldings, and rubble. Moving dressed stone required much attention (opposite) in order to avoid chipping the edges. The transport of rubble did not demand such care (below).

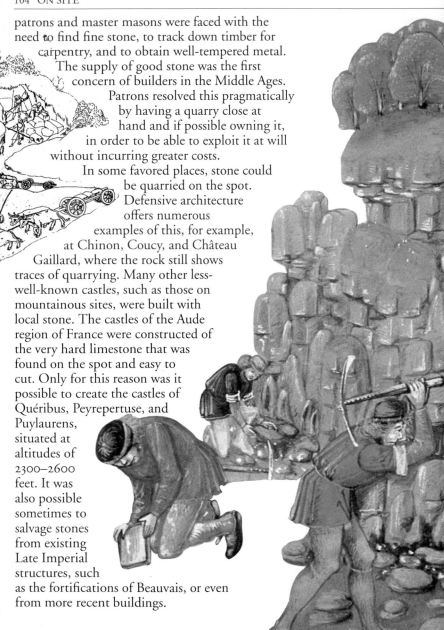

patrons and master masons were faced with the need to find fine stone, to track down timber for carpentry, and to obtain well-tempered metal.

The supply of good stone was the first concern of builders in the Middle Ages. Patrons resolved this pragmatically by having a quarry close at hand and if possible owning it, in order to be able to exploit it at will without incurring greater costs.

In some favored places, stone could be quarried on the spot. Defensive architecture offers numerous examples of this, for example, at Chinon, Coucy, and Château Gaillard, where the rock still shows traces of quarrying. Many other less-well-known castles, such as those on mountainous sites, were built with local stone. The castles of the Aude region of France were constructed of the very hard limestone that was found on the spot and easy to cut. Only for this reason was it possible to create the castles of Quéribus, Peyrepertuse, and Puylaurens, situated at altitudes of 2300–2600 feet. It was also possible sometimes to salvage stones from existing Late Imperial structures, such as the fortifications of Beauvais, or even from more recent buildings.

Quarries

Makeshift sources were no longer satisfactory when ambitions grew larger, and we find many mentions in manuscripts of patrons going to seek out hitherto unknown quarries or those where the workings had been abandoned. At the beginning of the 11th century, in order to reconstruct Cambrai Cathedral, Bishop Gérard I set off in search of a quarry which he finally found at Lesdain, some 6 miles away from Cambrai. Many other examples could be cited;

another patron, Abbot Suger, discovered quarries near Pontoise that could furnish stone for the monolithic columns in the ambulatory of St.-Denis. To reduce the cost, either the quarry had to be bought (as Chermizy was for Laon Cathedral) or a deal had to be concluded for the period of construction (as was done at Tours, Troyes, Meaux, Amiens, and elsewhere). In many cases, by good fortune, the quarries already belonged to the clergy (for instance Lyons and Chartres). However, quarries could also be in private hands and worked commercially, and this must have been the case in Paris, where there were stone outcrops on the slopes above the River Bièvre.

Stone was extracted from either an underground mine (opposite left) or an open quarry (opposite right). The cost was not the same, as mines had to be shored up with costly timber frames to avoid collapse. The quarryman's trade was a particularly dangerous one and required specialized knowledge, which was used in the choice of seams and in the calculation of the size of the blocks to be cut. Picks, miners' bars, and wooden wedges were the tools used to extract the undressed stone. It is understandable that for reasons of economy, the facing stones were plundered from accessible sections of fine earlier buildings. This exposed the rubble inside, as can be seen here at the Tomb of Cecilia Metella in Rome (left).

Because of their remoteness, these quarries presented huge problems and heavy costs.

England imported millions of tons of stone from Caen across the Channel very shortly after the Norman Conquest to construct the cathedral and the abbey church of St. Augustine at Canterbury, the royal palace of Westminster, the Tower of London, Battle Abbey, and much else, before other quarries were discovered near Stamford in Lincolnshire. The crucial question of transport remained, and William of Sens devised new ways of unloading stone from the boats that had carried it.

Transport of Heavy Material

Once barges had been invented, transport by water was the most practical and cheapest method. For Notre-Dame in Paris, they came down the Bièvre and took the minor branch of the Seine before discharging at the eastern end of the Ile de la Cité, near the cathedral building site. Streams and rivers were used

Stone was transported by water or land. By water, there were specially constructed flat-bottomed barges that would approach as close to the building site as possible (above). Overloading could lead to accidents. Although cheaper than transport by road, it was nevertheless inconvenient because of the need to load and unload twice.

On land, horses, and, to a greater degree, oxen, played a key role. Admiration grew for the ox, that strong and placid animal that plodded along the roads in the Middle Ages, and it was justly celebrated in stone by the architect of Laon Cathedral (left).

heavily; the Loire, for example, served to bring stone from the Nivernais to St.-Benoît-sur-Loire in Abbot Gauzlin's time. Elsewhere, as at Rievaulx and Bury St. Edmunds, special canals were built to avoid having to unload and reload.

Transport by road was sometimes unavoidable, but the shortest way was always sought. When the priory church at Poissy, near Paris, was built at the beginning of the 14th century, stone extracted from the quarries at Conflans was first transported down the Seine before being brought on site along tracks driven in a straight line through the vineyards.

Gradients posed a considerable problem. In order to carry stone from the quarry at Chermizy, 10 miles from Laon, to the summit of the *arx* (fortress) standing some 300 feet above the plain, it was necessary to use heavy carts drawn by oxen— creatures held in such high esteem that they were depicted on the cathedral towers.

The Middle Ages were particularly inventive in the matter of heavy haulage. The invention of the shoulder collar and the coupling of animals one behind the other in teams allowed horses to pull loads of 2.5 tons, when in antiquity they could haul only one-fifth as much. Horses could now draw almost as much as oxen, and they were half again as fast.

> "The image of the ox stands for strength and power, the ability to plow intellectual furrows that will receive the fruitful rains from heaven, while the horns symbolize invincible and protecting strength."
> Pseudo-Dionysius,
> c. AD 500

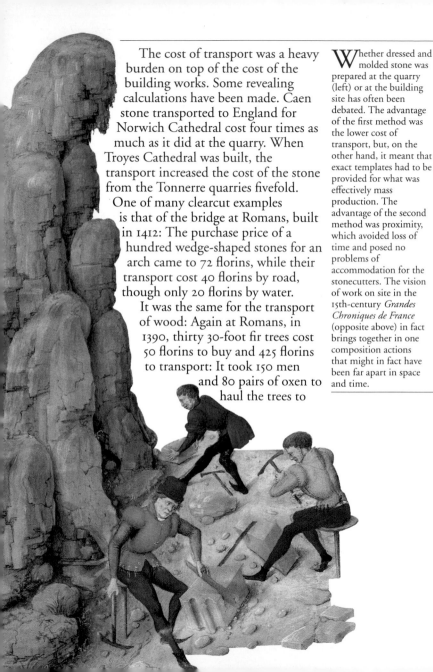

The cost of transport was a heavy burden on top of the cost of the building works. Some revealing calculations have been made. Caen stone transported to England for Norwich Cathedral cost four times as much as it did at the quarry. When Troyes Cathedral was built, the transport increased the cost of the stone from the Tonnerre quarries fivefold. One of many clearcut examples is that of the bridge at Romans, built in 1412: The purchase price of a hundred wedge-shaped stones for an arch came to 72 florins, while their transport cost 40 florins by road, though only 20 florins by water.

It was the same for the transport of wood: Again at Romans, in 1390, thirty 30-foot fir trees cost 50 florins to buy and 425 florins to transport: It took 150 men and 80 pairs of oxen to haul the trees to

Whether dressed and molded stone was prepared at the quarry (left) or at the building site has often been debated. The advantage of the first method was the lower cost of transport, but, on the other hand, it meant that exact templates had to be provided for what was effectively mass production. The advantage of the second method was proximity, which avoided loss of time and posed no problems of accommodation for the stonecutters. The vision of work on site in the 15th-century *Grandes Chroniques de France* (opposite above) in fact brings together in one composition actions that might in fact have been far apart in space and time.

Mortar was certainly mixed near the site (below) and transported immediately on a man's back before it had a chance to set. The quality of construction was judged by the mortar as much as by the stone.

the Isère river. In spite of these costs, waterways and tracks were traversed continually by barges and carts supplying the bustling building sites. The picture becomes even more vivid when one realizes that there were often several building sites close to each other in Normandy in the mid 11th century, in England at the end of the 11th century, and in the Ile-de-France in the second half of the 12th century.

Dressing Stone in the Quarries vs. Dressing It on Site

It is easy to understand that patrons sought to reduce costs by lightening the loads. Blocks came to be both roughed out and cut in the quarry, reviving an ancient custom and making the work easier.

Das die cristen entgiengen in das elsas kamen vnd gar grossen schaden taten

A 15th-Century Picture Story

If transport of materials was a problem, lifting them was an even greater one. Knowledge of machines invented by Roman architects had been lost, but at some unknown time it was rediscovered on very innovative building sites. Differences between regions were probably very great. *The Bern Chronicle* of 1484–5 by Diebold Schilling shows not only completed structures, like the town walls of Strasbourg, but the crane that stood on the roof of the still-unfinished cathedral (opposite). The artist also recorded various types of lifting devices, like the claw (left above) or the treadwheel crane that unloaded the barges (left below).

Pages 112–3: Other pictures in the manuscript illustrate different activities on the building site, including stonecutting, transport of rubble in horse-drawn carts, and laying of dressed stones with the aid of a claw.

Since William of Sens prepared templates and
sent them to Caen, there is much information on
the practice.

During the construction of Vale Royal Abbey
(between 1277 and 1298), masons were sent to the
quarries with their assistants to hew and cut a
thousand stones. It was the same for Westminster
Abbey in 1253. The stones dressed in this way were
the visible elements in
masonry: They included
not only facing, but also
jambs, tracery, and
moldings, which
explains the care
with which they
were chosen.

Wood and Carpentry

Carpentry posed equal
problems, increased by
severe deforestation that
had taken place in the
10th and 11th centuries.
Tall forest trees became
rare. In the 12th
century, Abbot Suger
recounted with self-
satisfaction how he had
miraculously discovered
wood essential for the
roof structure of St.-
Denis in the forest
of Yveline, although
experts had told him
it was not to be
found. (The
anecdote is quite
probably true.)

Sovereigns, lords,
bishops, and abbots

adopted a concerted policy of maintaining their forests. The Cistercians, seeking to enlarge their holdings, acted with particular care in this respect, and anarchy was followed by careful management. This did not mean that even in the 13th century architects were not in difficulties. Villard de Honnecourt was sufficiently aware of the problem to demonstrate how to build a bridge with short timbers.

In spite of the triumph of stone, wood remained indispensable. It was used structurally and also for scaffolding. In the middle of the 14th century, 3944 trees were needed to build Windsor Castle.

Patrons did not often own quarries, but they did own vast forests, at least in the north. They thus concerned themselves with better yields and a better product.

The building of the Ark, directed by Noah as architect, is depicted in the early-15th-century *Bedford Hours* (left) as the construction of a wooden house, with very precise representations of all the carpenters' tools, including plane, awls, and saw.

Another illumination (above) shows trees being cut down and timbers being shaped for a wooden bridge and a roof.

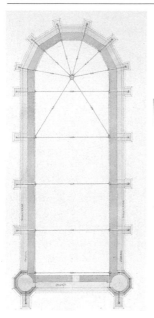

The Ste.-Chapelle in Paris, finished in 1248, is tied together at the upper level by two metal chains that encircle it and by metal tie-rods stretched between the buttresses and concealed within the roof.

Transverse rods are linked by a tensioning connector; in the apse, a multiple connector receives eight tie-rods. Finally, there are longitudinal chains. In the lower chapel, metal tie-rods link the colonnettes and the exterior walls; the ribs in the apse are themselves reinforced by metal bars that follow their shape. The architect who restored the Ste.-Chapelle in the 19th century took care to record the arrangement in plan (left, the upper chapel). He also drew the multiple connector (above).

Metal, an Essential Building Material

Less is known about the third building material, metal. Mastery of its processes, from extraction in a mine to its use in the final cutting of the stone, has much to do with the progress of architecture. The quality of stonecutting necessarily depended on that of the tools—on their sharpness and on the temper of the metal, making them more resistant to wear. Here again there were considerable differences between one region and another, and between one building site and another, as acquired habits were not easily challenged. The appearance of the specialized stonecutter's hammer in the north during the 12th century was a kind of revolution that some took advantage of more than others.

The quality of Cistercian architecture from the 1120s on is related to the order's technological inventiveness. They placed importance on metal, both the extraction of ore and its subsequent processing. At the abbey of Fontenay the forge is not outside, as one might reasonably expect, but inside the monastic enclosure—metalworking was thus part of the activity of the monks and not of the lay brothers. This spirit accounted for progress that appeared in spheres other than building, and particularly in agriculture.

It is probable that this experiment spread rapidly as in fact Gothic architecture cannot be understood otherwise. Moreover, metal became an essential element in Rayonnant architecture, when buildings like the Ste.-Chapelle in Paris were conceived with a system of iron reinforcements. This type of construction in reinforced stone, which calls to mind the

Metal had been used intensively by Gothic architects well before the advent of the Rayonnant style. The oldest evidence is in Soissons Cathedral, in the south transept (c. 1170). The collegiate church at St.-Quentin (left) had tie-rods situated well above the springing of the vault. They served to contain the thrust of the vaults. A tensioning connector in the center allowed them to be tightened or slackened, and they played just as significant a role as the flying buttresses. The tie-rods in the apse were removed at the end of the last century, but those in the nave were retained; after shelling in the First World War, the apse vaults collapsed, while in the nave the ribs survived and only the webs were damaged. When the church was restored after that disaster, the tie-rods in the nave were removed.

reinforced concrete of the beginning of the 20th century, demanded a substantial supply of metal and thus of iron ore. Where did it come from in the 13th century? In the 15th century, there is much evidence to show that the metal was imported from Spain at extremely high prices. Whether the same was true earlier is a question that cannot at present be answered.

Machines

After materials, the last element involved in construction is machines and the physical help they provide. Inventions were made in this area, as elsewhere in the Middle Ages; and where machines are found to be based on older types, as they often were, engineers were able to analyze, perfect, and simplify them. Machines already existed in antiquity, when they were the focus of much attention, but in the Middle Ages they became indispensable as huge buildings were undertaken without the help of slaves. The study of medieval techniques is

Mariano Taccola, born in Siena in 1381, produced *De Machinis Libri Decem* (Ten Books on Machines) in 1449. He was no more a practical inventor than Leonardo da Vinci, but he was an inspired compiler who had a sense for the visual. His captions explaining the machines (left) are somewhat naive, for example: "Let us suppose that it is a question of raising a bell to a belfry or tower by means of a winch or a hoist. So that the bell may be raised with greater ease, a crate filled with stone is put on the other side. And as the bell goes up, the crate comes down."

difficult because of the absence of texts on the subject and the fact that images, while abundant, are repetitive. One can never be sure that the painters, illuminators, or draftsmen who depicted a construction site were copying from reality. A number of them, moreover, show the Tower of Babel, which is in the realm of mythology. Nor do the images represent up-to-date methods; they are nearly always out of phase. There are indeed some pictures that are a straight transcription of a specific event, but they are the exception and allow us to follow the rapidity of the development.

Less than 150 years separate the Battle of Hastings —and the Bayeux Tapestry—from the long wars waged by the Plantagenets (Henry II, Richard II, John) against the Capetians (Philip Augustus). The difference is as great as that between trench warfare at the beginning of the 20th century and the highly developed technology used in the Gulf War of 1992. This gap, which has always to be borne in mind in studies of the Middle Ages, is essential to the understanding of this period.

Taccola's explanation of the double cart, also called the great truck (below), is not entirely based on reality, and it is clear that devices in common use were not always comprehensible. His manuscript demonstrates the fascination exercised over men of this period by the technical means that had made great architectural achievements possible. A 10th-century Greek manuscript (above left) shows the sort of model Taccola might have had for his idea of raising a column by means of a winch.

The Architectural Advantages of Warfare

War, it has often been said, encourages the use of previously unknown resources. It promotes rationalization, as much in the political as in the architectural sphere. From the second half of the 12th century, machines were invented to besiege cities or fortresses. The greatest innovation was the trebuchet (also known as perrier or mangonel), which hurled stones by means of a counterweight system. Experiments have shown that a trebuchet manned by 50 people and with a counterweight of 10 tons was capable of hurling a 200–300 pound stone a distance of 500 feet, compared with a Roman catapult which threw a 45–55 pound stone about 750 feet.

The siege laid for several months by Philip Augustus to Château Gaillard, which finally fell, was maintained by a series of actions in which machines played a great part, some of it psychological. It is at this period that we begin to find the names of engineers responsible for devising war machines whose construction called for experts in carpentry. There were immediate consequences for the civilian world.

Cranes and Scaffolding

Lifting devices were in current use in antiquity. The Roman writer Vitruvius, whose book on building was well known in the Middle Ages, gave a reasonably clear explanation of them. In the Middle Ages they were greatly improved, owing particularly to the use of the counterweight and double pulleys. The crane

The distinction between machines for military and civilian use is not always easy to establish, since the engineer might serve a prince both in war and in the production of works of monumental art. The construction of wooden mantlets or armored cars (above) utilized classic carpentry techniques.

stood directly on the ground if the buildings were not too tall; otherwise it was placed on a platform. It was made in such a way that assembly and dismantling required only a small crew of men. In addition, some cranes pivoted; the overhang of the boom could be as much as 10 feet; and pulleys arranged in sequence could function as a gear mechanism. Various means were used to power the cranes, the simplest being the windlass, whose power was necessarily limited. Then came the treadwheel, also used in antiquity, which was worked by two men walking inside the wheel, or rotating it by pulling on ladder-like bars on the outer surface. It has been calculated that with a wheel 8 feet in diameter, a man could raise a weight roughly 1200–1300 pounds. Here again the technicians of the Middle Ages proved themselves to be very inventive, enlarging the wheels up to a diameter of 26 feet, doubling their size, and increasing the number of workers. Making treadwheels was simple, which explains why they were set up on top of vaults—where

Conrad Keyser, engineer of King Sigismund of Hungary at the end of the 14th century, compiled a work illustrated with particularly sophisticated machines, such as this one (left), which made use both of a crane and a horizontal beam. Inspired by a military machine, it was meant to bore through the length of tree trunks to make pipes.

The elaborate combination of treadwheel and crane (above) was no doubt also linked to the progress of military technology in the second half of the 12th century.

some survive to this day, for instance at Beauvais, Châlons-sur-Marne, and some churches in Alsace. There was no hesitation in moving them about and adapting them to different roles. The one at Châlons-sur-Marne Cathedral, originally on the first western bay of the nave, above the oculus in the center of the vault, was reduced in size and moved to the space above the north transept.

The use of these lifting devices had an important effect on the character of scaffolding. In the Romanesque period, scaffolding was heavy, resting on the ground and fixed into the masonry by horizontal poles. It was used in the making of stone vaults. Planks laid on these vertical and horizontal elements constituted both the masons' working platform and a storage space for materials. The scaffolding therefore had to be very solid, and access to it was gained by movable wooden ladders used by the masons and the carriers of stones and mortar.

As in antiquity, machines for raising weights were extremely simple, consisting of the crane and the treadwheel. With the former, as a miniature shows (left), a hook was sufficient for modest weights, while for heavier weights, a claw was needed. The 15th-century illuminator was in error about the mechanics: The ropes should have been pulled from the ground, not from the top of the tower. The treadwheel was easy to construct. It could be dismantled and set up again as building progressed, ending up in the roof, where a number are still in existence. The one at the base of the spire of Salisbury Cathedral (opposite left), dates from the 14th century and is still in working order. Another is shown being used at the top of the Tower of Babel in a 15th-century book of hours (opposite right).

From Solid to Void

The birth of Gothic architecture is connected with the arrival of lifting devices that allowed materials to be raised directly to the wall. This was a revolutionary step. Scaffolding no longer served as a surface on which to put material, but as the working platform of the individual mason. It thus became considerably

Philippe FIX

This modern illustration of a cathedral under construction gives a clear idea of a Gothic building site. Note the huge scale of the building and the variety of activities in different places, for instance in the western crypt (bottom right). From this image we can understand at a glance all the stages of the building, which normally progressed from east to west—from the choir to the facade—and from the foundations up to the roof. One detail is inaccurate: The crossing and aisle would have been protected by roofs before the stone vaults were begun.

lighter. The technique of suspending scaffolding from the wall, rather than resting it on the ground, was rediscovered. Access to upper working levels was made easier by spiral staircases within the masonry which the architect built first to enable the workers to climb more easily. Horizontal circulation was made possible by narrow passages built inside the thick walls. The construction of rib vaults called for scaffolding that did not rest on the ground but projected from wall to wall, providing particularly large work surfaces and also facilitating the handling of heavy timber centering. Finally—the ultimate advance—the scaffolding could be easily taken down and used again, according to the needs and progress of the construction site.

A True Partnership

High technology of this kind was to be seen only on the construction sites of great cathedrals and abbeys and major secular buildings. Everything was different for less important projects. There, techniques remained traditional in the use and handling of stone. The gap between cathedral and village church is

almost the same as that which can be seen today between the most sophisticated modern office building and a garden shed. Not to realize this is to run the risk of making grave errors in assessment.

Scaffolding was a major concern for Gothic architects, and they sought to simplify it and make it lighter (below, the construction of an abbey in the 15th century).

Architects of the Middle Ages were curiously similar to architects of the Renaissance, the 18th century, and even of the modern world. Strictly tied to the patrons who hired them, they tried to satisfy the patrons' ambition. On their own, they remained mere dreamers. Their genius could be liberated only when they met a patron who challenged them to put concepts into practice, to realize them. Architecture is born of this duality: patron plus architect.

Opposite: A 15th-century artist depicted the structure of the Church as a building site, complete with accurately drawn tools. The arrangement is hierarchical. The two laborers are Cain and Abel; starting from the bottom, we move from patriarchs up to prophets, on to kings, princes, and judges, then to apostles (setting the glazing in place) and martyrs, and finally to the confessors, who are finishing the roof.

Overleaf: A 15th-century building site.

DOCUMENTS

Careful examination of medieval buildings
reveals little or nothing about the techniques used
or the organization of the building site. For this
we can turn to pictures—which are generally
late in date and sometimes based on stereotypes—
or written documents. These records are plentiful
but sometimes difficult to understand,
and most have been relatively
little used and rarely translated.

The Architect

At the beginning of the 11th century, patrons—clerics or not—could not find architects already capable of realizing their grand visions and found that it was necessary to train them. After a generation, these master masons became professionals and were the object of suspicion and jealousy.

I n medieval illuminations the architect is represented holding a measuring rod, dividers, or a set square.

Works of Abbot Thierry, Successor to Airard, at St.-Remi at Reims (Anselm, *Historia*, 1039)

Abbot Airard began a colossal building, so exceptional for its time that he could not see it through to completion. His successor, Thierry, decided to destroy much of the work that had been done and replace it with something more realistic.

In the year 1005, Airard, inspired by the example of a great number of famous prelates of his time, decided to renew the church he had in his care. He summoned renowned architects and began, from the foundations, an edifice in dressed stone. It was to be much more elegant and magnificent than any then being built in France, but for this reason neither he nor his contemporaries would see it completed. Having fulfilled his functions as abbot for about twenty-eight years, he died ripe in years, without having been able to finish his work.

After his death, Thierry, his successor, wished to finish his undertaking; but the task was so enormous it seemed impossible for him to bring it to a successful conclusion. He therefore took counsel of the wisest of the monks subordinate to him, and of the most worthy people in the province of Reims. On their advice he decided on the partial destruction of his predecessor's building, while keeping some foundations whose retention appeared necessary to the architects. Then he began the construction of a simpler but equally suitable church.

It was the fifth year since his promotion to the position of abbot, about 1039, when he undertook this work. Laymen and clergy tried to outdo each other in helping him;

several members of the clergy of their own accord used their carts and their oxen for the transport of materials. Foundations were dug where there had been none before, columns from the first, destroyed building were placed upon them, carefully centered arches were built above them, and the basilica began to take shape in the hands of the builders. Then when the gallery walls had been built everywhere and the ridge of the nave had risen to its greatest height, the old church dedicated by Hincmar in ancient times was razed to the ground. A temporary roof was erected over the monks' choir, so that they could attend divine services without being exposed to the weather.

In the midst of all this, in 1045 Abbot Thierry died prematurely after governing his monastery for eleven years and eight months. Herimar, his successor, had been provost of the abbey; in that capacity he had already been one of Thierry's most enthusiastic collaborators in the building of the church and had given him many subsidies from the revenue of the domains he administered. Hence he did not leave the work of his predecessor in abeyance for long: he completed the south transept, which was already in an advanced state, and also the north, of which only the foundations and the staircases leading to the upper parts yet existed. Finally, with great beams brought from the neighboring forest of Orbais Abbey, he raised a timber roof over the building, which was then completed in every part.

Victor Mortet, *Recueil de Textes Relatifs à l'Histoire de l'Architecture…*, 1911

Construction of Salisbury Cathedral by Bishop Roger (William of Malmesbury, *De Gestis Regum Anglorum,* 1107)

Roger, the Norman bishop of Salisbury, introduced French techniques and style into England.

The bishop was a generous man and never considered the expense when he decided what he ought to do, especially when he was carrying out building projects. This can be seen in many places, but especially at Salisbury and Malmesbury. At Malmesbury he had great structures built, hugely expensive and of very beautiful appearance. The coursing was so precisely realized that the fit of the stones struck the eye and gave the illusion that all the masonry was made up of a single stone. As for Salisbury Cathedral, the bishop had it restored and decorated so richly that it was second to none in England and indeed surpassed many. He could honestly say to God: "Lord, I have loved the beauty of thy dwelling."

Victor Mortet, *Recueil de Textes Relatifs à l'Histoire de l'Architecture…*, 1911

The Building of Lincoln Cathedral by Bishop Hugh

The Metrical Life of St. Hugh *is a long poem in Latin hexameters probably written in the 1220s, around the time of Hugh's canonization (he died in 1200). For the poet, a cathedral is a spiritual entity. Its significance resides in the level of symbolism and allegory that it can be made to yield. He is quite uninterested in the practical side of building, and if Lincoln Cathedral did not exist, it would be hard to reconstruct it from his description. On the other hand, he does convey something of the power and meaning which it must have had for his contemporaries, and which is largely a closed book to us today.*

With wonderful art he built the work that is the cathedral church. For in its erection he not only granted means and the labour of his own servants, but the aid of his own sweat. Many a time he carried the hewn stones in a kind of hod, and the lime-mortar also. A handicapped man who was lame and propped on two crutches had the task of carrying that hod assigned to him, believing there must be good presage in it—and thereafter he disdained the help of his two crutches. The day's work, which tends to make the straight crooked, made his crookedness straight....

The old mass of masonry was completely demolished and a new one rose. Its state as it rose fitly expressed the form of a cross. By arduous labour its three parts are integrated into one. The very solid mass of the foundation goes up from the middle, the wall carries the roof high into the air. The foundation is thus buried in the bowels of the earth, but wall and roof lie open, as with proud boldness the wall soars up towards the clouds, and the roof towards the stars. The costliness of the material is well matched by [the] zeal of the craftsmanship. The vault seems to converse with the winged birds; it spreads broad wings of its own, and like a flying creature jostles the clouds, while yet resting upon its

St. Hugh's choir, Lincoln.

solid pillars. The gripping mortar glues the white stones together, all of which the mason's hand has hewn true to the mark. But although the wall is put together from the mass of separate stones, it seems to disdain this fact and gives the semblance of joining in a continuum the contiguous parts. It seems to be the result not of art but of nature, not a thing unified but a single entity. The work is supported by another costly material consisting of black stonework [Purbeck marble], as though it is not content with thus having just one colour.... On being closely inspected this stone can hold people's minds in suspense as they wonder whether it is jasper or marble; but if jasper, then dull jasper, while if marble, an aristocrat of marbles. Of this substance are the shafts, which encircle the pillars in such a way that they seem to be keeping up a kind of ring-dance there. Their outer surface, more polished than a fresh-growing fingernail, presents a starry brilliance to the dazzled sight, for nature has painted there so many varied forms that, if art should toil with sustained endeavour to produce a similar painting, it could hardly copy what nature has done. Thus handsome jointing arranges there in seemly rank a thousand shafts which, strong, precious, and gleaming, render the whole structure of the cathedral durable with their strength while enriching it with their costliness and brightening it with their gleam. For the shafts themselves stand soaring and lofty, their finish is clear and resplendent, their order graceful

and geometrical, their beauty fit and serviceable, their function gratifying and excellent, their rigid strength undecayingly sharp to the touch.

The resplendent procession of windows on the two sides confronts the eyes with puzzles to be worked out. The sequence has depicted on it citizens of the Celestial City and the weapons with which they overcame the Stygian tyrant. And there are two larger windows, like two luminaries;

their circular radiance, looking to north and south, outshines all the other windows with these twin lustres. The others are comparable to common stars, but these two are, the one like the sun, and the other like the moon. Thus two candelabra make the upper reaches of the cathedral bright, with their vivid and various colours imitating the rainbow: indeed, not imitating but surpassing; for the sun, when it is reflected on the clouds, produces the rainbow, whereas those two windows gleam without the sun and flash without clouds....

The foundation is the body, the wall is the man, the roof is the spirit; the division of the church is thus threefold. The body has as its portion earth, the man has the clouds, the spirit has the stars....

Illuminating the world with heavenly light is the distinguished band of the clergy, and this is expressed by the bright windows. There is a ranking order on either side, which can be remarked: in the clerestory range the rank of canon, and in the aisle range that of vicar. And since, while a canon is handling the world's affairs, his vicar is perpetually and diligently carrying out the divine offices, the top range of windows shines illustrious with flower-petals, signifying the varied beauty of the world, while the lower range presents the names of the holy fathers. The twin windows that offer a circular light are the two Eyes of the cathedral; and rightly the greater of these is seen to be the bishop and the lesser the dean. For north represents the devil, and south the Holy Spirit and it is in these directions that the two Eyes look. The bishop faces the south in order to invite in, and the dean the

north in order to avoid; the one takes care to be saved, the other takes care not to perish. With these Eyes the cathedral's face is on the watch for the candelabra of heaven and the darkness of Lethe.

The Metrical Life of St. Hugh
Translated by Charles Gaston, 1986

Contract of the Master Mason Gautier de Varinfroy for Meaux Cathedral (1253)

Contracts binding patrons and master masons came into common use in the 13th century.

The bishop, dean, and chapter of Meaux send greetings in God to all those who read this letter. We hereby announce that we have entrusted to Master Gautier de Varinfroy of the diocese of Meaux direction of the building works of our church under the following conditions: He is to receive ten *livres* each year, as long as we ourselves, our successors and the said chapter allow him to work on the said site. In the event of him falling long and continuously ill so that he could no longer work, he is not to receive the said ten *livres*. He is also to receive three *sous* a day while working on the building site, or when he is sent on errands in connection with the works. In addition, he cannot accept any work outside the diocese without our permission. Over and above this, he will receive wood from the building site which cannot be used there. He will not have the right to go to the site at Evreux or to any other site outside Meaux, or to remain there longer than two months, without the permission of the chapter of Meaux. He will be obliged to live in the town of

Meaux and he has sworn that he will work faithfully on the above-named building site and will remain loyal to it. Drawn up in the year of Our Lord 1253 in the month of October.

Roland Recht, *Les Bâtisseurs des Cathédrales Gothiques*, 1989

Fortification of Ardres by Arnoul II, Count of Guines: The Role of Master Simon and the Workers on the Building Site (1200–1)

The problem of professional status arose as soon as there was a demand for specialized architects.

Arnoul II, count of Guines, resolved to fortify Ardres in imitation of the walls (*fossatum*) protecting St.-Omer. He surrounded the town with a protective wall, the likes of which had never been made by arms nor seen by eyes in the whole land of Guines. A large number of workers were gathered to make and dig out the moat. The geometer Master Simon, directing the work, and walking as a master with his measuring rod, as was the custom, here and there measured the work that had already been planned in his mind, less with his measuring rod than by eye. He had houses and barns demolished; he cut down orchards, flowering trees, and fruit trees; he pulled down many buildings that had formerly been made available to travelers at great expense; he broke up gardens of vegetables and flax; he destroyed and beat down the fields to make roads. He did not bother about those who became angry and cried out, nor about those who grumbled silently about him. The peasants, given blocks and tackles, used wagons for transporting marl and used dung carts

The choir of Meaux Cathedral.

to bring stones to spread on the roads. The trench diggers were seen working with their hoes, the diggers with their spades, the pioneers with their picks, the demolition men with their mallets, the road workers and the levelers with their trenching tools, the workmen working on the facing, the beaters (who rammed down the soil), each with the equipment and instruments that were most suitable and necessary for them. Carriers and porters were to be seen, and the turfers with long pieces of sod that had been cut and lifted from the meadows on the master's orders. The sergeants and the lord's agents, armed with knotty sticks, called out at times to the workmen, and at times urged them on to do the work in the manner that the foremen, who preceded them, had carefully laid down.

Gabriel Fournier
Le Château dans la France Médiévale
1978

The Building Site

Building sites are often depicted in late medieval illuminations, but we have little sense of what they were really like. There are very few documents that can resurrect this rich, living, and vivid world for us.

S eal of the Strasbourg masons' lodge in the 16th century.

Construction of Noyers Castle (*Gesta Pontificum Autissiodorensium,* 1106–1206)

The author of the Acts of the Bishops of Auxerre *describes in minute detail the construction of a castle.*

We have thought it useful to describe the works which Hugues de Noyers carried out at the castle (*castrum*) of Noyers, which is part of his heritage and which has been made famous through the deeds of his ancestors…and to describe the efforts he has made for the improvement of the fortifications of that place and the considerable expenditure he has made there. At the top of the walls of the lower town, situated at the bottom of the mountain and bathed on every side by the Serein River, he built solid firing devices in masonry or very strong wood. On the mountain slope above the town, although the castle (*castrum*) was inaccessible from this quarter owing to the nature of the site, he set about creating trenches dug deep into the mountain rock, as well as fortified gateways. Higher up, at the top of the mountain where the central part of the fortress (*presidium*) stands, a large area was prepared to make a site suitable for the installation of war machines. In addition to the ancient walls of the castle (*munitio*)—of which the outer one was solid (it had been built by Bishop Clérembaud's brother shortly before his death)—he erected another, higher wall behind the interior one, which was thicker and stronger, and in the middle he built a strong tower (*turris*). Along the outer wall he made deep trenches, digging out the rock, and in front of that he had further

On the construction site, it was crucial to coordinate the work of the different trades.

excavations made in the mountain to keep the enemy away from the principal part of the fortress (*presidium*) by numerous obstacles and barriers. He made projections in the outer wall; their upper part was covered with beams of extreme thickness. Those inside, therefore, need not fear missiles, no matter how heavy, nor catapults nor any other devices of the enemy, but in safety they would deny access to the trenches to any assailants coming from the front, as well as access to the wall to which these defenses were attached. Outside the ramparts of the principal part of the fortress (*presidium principale*), he constructed a palace (*palatium*) of great beauty, which completed the defenses of the principal part of the fortress (*presidium munitionis*). It was a pleasant lordly residence, which he decorated with taste with numerous ornaments. He had subterranean passages made leading from the wine cellar—which lay beneath the tower (*turris principalis*)—to the palace situated lower down, so that to get wine and other provisions it would not be necessary to go in or out of the principal part of the fortress. While provisions were let down in baskets to the foot of the wall of the central part of the fortress, wine and water [were conveyed], with great care, through lead pipes that were very cleverly fashioned. Thus supplies assembled for the castle garrison were kept there under heavy guard and in complete safety, and after protecting them with bars to make them safe from all threat, they were able to serve and satisfy all needs on demand. Furthermore, he equipped the principal part of the fortress (*presidium*) with weapons, war machines, and other devices necessary for defense. At great expense, he bought the houses of the knights and others which lay within the ramparts of the upper fortress (*munitio*) and he reassigned the property to his nephew. Thus, both in this part of the fortress and in the main building of the palace, as a measure of safety, the arrival of those who wanted to see the lord in his palace (*palatium*), situated outside the surrounding wall of the principal part of the fortress (*principale presidium*), would not arouse suspicion. And since any non-resident could be excluded in time of danger, the lord of the castle was no longer forced to let any man enter the upper ramparts (*infra septa superiora*) without being sure of his allegiance. Also for this reason he moved the parish church of the locality (*municipium*) outside the walls (*extra septa*), allowing only a chapel for the lord within the upper part [of the fortress].

Victor Mortet, *Recueil de Textes Relatifs à l'Histoire de l'Architecture...*, 1911

Accounts for the Work Done at the Collège de Beauvais in Paris by the Executors of Jean de Dormans (1387)

This document perfectly evokes everyday life on the building site: advertising the work to be done and calling for bids, site meetings, and payment of the workers.

Item, to apply and execute the said decision and order of our said lords, shortly afterwards the said Master Raymon [of the Temple] made and set out a report detailing the form, the materials, the style, and the thickness of the said building, and had it copied by his clerk, so that the work and the specification should be known by all the warranted and competent workers who would care to make and execute this work at a lower price.... Several working masons, having seen the report and taken note of it, bid for the said work and several times lowered their asking price. Nevertheless, after much barter and many discussions, the said contract, for its better profit and greater utility, according to the opinion and

Where there was no good building stone, brick was used for structural purposes.

decision of the said Master Raymon, was awarded to and remained with the first masons whose prices had already been reduced, and who were at work every day, while waiting for any who might close the said deal for a lower price, as has been said....

On Thursday, feast day of the beheading of St. John, Master Raymon came to the workshop and saw the masons, the hewers, and the others... he examined minutely and measured all the excavations from the base up to ground level....

Because stones from Gentilly were arriving in great numbers in several carts, there was no time to examine them properly; a poor stonecutter who was always in the workshop was assigned to check whether they were satisfactory, and, for this work, he was given, *ex gratia*...four *sous*....

At the time of this work, in summer, since the days were long and it was hot and they were bringing stones, lime, sand, and other materials, several times it was advisable to give water to those who were working to stop them grumbling....

On Friday eighteenth day of October, it was the feast-day of St. Luke, and although on this day all work should cease according to the commandments of the Church...the workshop was nevertheless kept at work....

Let it be known that one day among others, while the foundations of the said walls were being laid, being the time when the frosts were coming and the season when masonry could be done was coming to an end, some of the masons, while they were going to lunch, asked and prayed that while they were taking their hour lunch break, the hewers should continue to work. The said hewers...wanted to have their hour's break in the same way. So they gave the said hewers food and drink in the trench itself so that they went on working without any interruption; for this...four *sous*.

On the day of Lent, when the masons and laborers were in the workshop, they demanded all together that, according to the custom in workshops where work is continuous, all the workmen and laborers should be given a favor, that is the meat of one sheep which they would all eat together....

Around Whitsuntide, the masons and laborers in the workshop who worked there permanently asked all with one voice as a mark of favor and kindness, which is the custom on every established and continuously working site like this one...whether they could eat together on the day of the Ascension of Our Lord and receive an advance on the expenses of the said workshop. The said Master Raymon, being the employer and master of the corps of masons and of all the laborers and their judge in this matter, wished to decide this...and so he decided...that if it pleased the said College to do thus and not otherwise, the said masons and laborers would dine together.... There came to this meal the said Master Raymon, as their employer, as well as his wife and several well-known and honorable persons....

Around the twentieth day of July, M. de Beauvais passed through this workshop, visited the workers, and inspected the work; he commanded his steward to give the workers a tip of one franc each.

Gustave Fagniez, *Etudes sur l'Industrie et la Classe Industrielle à Paris au XIIIe et au XIVe Siècles*, 1877

Materials

In order to construct buildings comparable to the monuments of ancient times, it was essential to find seams of fine stone that could be easily extracted and cut. For the timber needed in the carpentry work, it was necessary to plant seedlings and wait until the trees matured.

Bricks were manufactured on site for convenience and economy.

Construction of Battle Abbey, Near Hastings (*Chronicum Monasterii de Bello*, 1066)

Transport of materials was one of the concerns of the patron and the master mason. In England, stone was scarce, and it had to be imported from Normandy.

Since at the time the king was worried about the transport of building materials, the same monks suggested to him that the place where he had decided to build the church, being on a hill, was on soil that was arid, dried out, and without water; and that for these reasons it was advisable, if he thought fit, to choose a more suitable location for a work of such importance. When the king heard this, he was indignant and left immediately, commanding that the foundations of the sanctuary should be laid more rapidly still on the precise spot where his victory had been acknowledged after he had killed his enemy. And as the monks, who did not dare to oppose him, used the lack of water as a pretext, the magnanimous king replied, it is said, to their objections with these memorable words: "If by the grace of God my life is spared, I shall see the abbey established on this very spot, supplied with wine in greater quantity than any other major abbey is supplied with water." The monks again began to complain of the poor location, saying that no suitable building stone was to be found anywhere in the area for some distance, all the ground being covered by forests. So the king offered to meet all the costs by drawing on his own resources, and he even sent his ships to transport stone from the town of Caen by sea in sufficient quantity for the projected work. And when the monks, following the king's decisions, had transported part of the stone from Normandy by boat, it is said that at the same moment a nun had a revelation: If they dug in a place revealed to her in her vision, they would find a great quantity of stone for the projected work. So they went and looked, as they had been commanded to do, and not far from the area designated for the church they discovered stone in such rich quantity and quality that evidently a treasure had been buried there in former times by the will of God in order to provide the material for the intended building. At last the foundations were laid of this work which was of great importance in the eyes of the times and then, following the king's decision, the high altar was carefully sited on the very spot where King Harold's ensign, known as the "standard," had been seen to fall.

Victor Mortet, *Recueil de Textes Relatifs à l'Histoire de l'Architecture…* 1911

The Search for Wood for St.-Denis (Abbot Suger, *De Consecratione*, 1140)

The best-known text on the subject of the difficulty of finding wood is by Abbot Suger, patron of St.-Denis.

In order to find the beams, we consulted all those who work with wood in our area as well as in Paris, and they all replied that, in their opinion, because of the lack of forests, beams could not be found in these

The architect's first priority was to find stone and timber, here for the construction of Bern in the 12th century.

regions, but we should have to get them from the region of Auxerre. They were unanimous in that view; as for us, we were overwhelmed at the prospect of all the effort and the great delay that this would involve. One night, having returned from matins, I thought as I lay on my bed that I should myself go around the neighboring woods, and look everywhere to see whether I could find the beams and avoid the delay and the extra work. And so, putting aside all my other cares, I set off early in the morning with the carpenters and the dimensions of the beams and made my way quickly to the forest of Yveline. Passing through our lands in the valley of the Chevreuse, I called together our officials and those who were in charge of the land and all those who knew the forests well, and I asked them to say under oath whether we had any chance of finding beams of these dimensions in that area. They began to smile, and certainly would have burst out laughing if they could have, astonished that we should not know that nothing of that size was to be found in all those lands, especially since Milo, the Lord of Chevreuse, who was our vassal and who held half the forest in addition to another fief, and who for a long time had waged war with the king and Amaury de Montfort, had left nothing untouched or in a good state, having himself built three-storied defensive towers. We ourselves rejected everything that these men said, and with bold confidence we set out through the forest; in about an hour we found one beam of the right dimensions. What more was needed? At about nones or a little earlier, pushing our way through the woodland, through the thick forest, and through the thorn bushes, to the astonishment of all those present, who were gathered together, we discovered twelve beams. It was the number that we needed. We had them carried to the holy basilica and placed them with joy on the roof of the new work, to the praise and glory of the Lord Jesus who had procured them thus for himself and his martyrs, having chosen to protect them from the hands of robbers.

Abbot Suger
De Consecratione, 1140

Contract Made with Master Jean de Lohes, Mason, for the Building of the Castle at Bapaume in Flanders (1311)

Some contracts are extremely precise in specifying every detail.

To all those who will see and hear the present letters, greetings from Thomas Brandon, bailiff of Arras. May all know that the mason Jehan [Jean] de Lohes has appeared in person before us and before the men of Madame d'Artois, that is Master Girart de Saleu, Jehan Testart, and Jehan d'Estainbourg, and that he has acknowledged that he is to make for the castle of Madame d'Artois at Bapaume the masonry for a hall which will be 80 feet long and 70 feet wide on the inside. All around, there will be walls 5 feet thick and 40 feet high. On one side, there will be an arch adjoining the chapel as is suitable with an opening equal to the width of the chapel. The arch will be decorated with roll moldings; there will be four large windows at the ends of this hall, and four on the two sides, if as many are desired, as wide as is necessary. And there will be six double windows and six ordinary ones with frames on the inside. There will be two fireplaces in this hall, wherever it is wished they should be put. In the middle of the hall, lengthwise, there will be two freestanding columns and two attached to the wall, which will support three [transverse] arches in due manner, as high as they can be below the roof timbers, the spandrels of these arches being entirely masonry right up to the roofing. This central [transverse] wall will be 40 feet high like the others. The walls all around and the central wall will have entablatures both inside and outside, as is suitable. The aforesaid columns will be given bases and capitals. At the ends of the hall, there will be two gable ends as high and as wide as is necessary for them to fit the roof structure well. These gables will be crowned with French copings, as is suitable, and decorated on these copings with bosses, balls, and fleurons in sufficient quantity. At the four corners of the hall there will be turrets, as wide as is necessary, and a fifth turret in the center, on the courtyard side. The four corner turrets will spring from the entablature, while the other will spring from the ground; inside there will be a spiral staircase leading up to the wall passages. All around the said hall, there will be crenellated wall passages, with walkways which will allow people to come and go. The two gables will be set back inward so that the wall passages will be outside the gable ends as they should be. In this hall there will be as many door frames as is desired. The four turrets will be as high as the wall passages, and will be crenellated like the rest of the building. If it were desired to raise the turrets 10 feet above the passages, it should be done, and entablatures made all around so that the roof timbers could rest on them, if that is what is wished. The four columns in the hall will be of sandstone; the said Jehan is to furnish them at his own expense, except for the transport, the copings, and the capitals being worked with bosses and leaves. The two freestanding columns will be all of one piece, 15 feet long if that length is suitable and 18 spans in thickness; the two half-columns will be made of stone blocks and bonded to the walls. There will be as many gargoyles as are necessary for drainage purposes and, on the gables, as many openings as there should be. For the foundations, the said Jehan must go at his own expense 3 feet down below the ground; if it should prove necessary to go deeper, that would be at Madame's expense.

All that is said and estimated above is to be done by the said Jehan de Lohes at his own expense, for the workers as well as for the work, for the consideration of three hundred *livres parisis* [livres of Paris], which he will receive for the said work. All the materials are to be provided on the site: to wit stone, lime, sand, fencing, pulleys, rope, and whatever is necessary to this work. He is to provide labor to put up the fencing, and furnish the four columns at his own expense, as has been said, except for the transport, which will be charged to us. If the cost of the said work exceeds [the agreed cost] by ten *livres parisis*, nothing of that will be paid to the said Jehan, but he must work for the agreed salary; if the excess were more than ten *livres parisis*, he will be paid this on top of his salary, with an exemption of ten *livres*. The said Jehan must take the cut stone that is already available to use for the said work, and that at the price obtaining before work commences; he is to deduct this price from his salary. He is to finish the said work in a correct and satisfactory manner in the present season, if he can.

Jules-Marie Richard,
Mahaut, Comtesse d'Artois et de Bourgogne (1302–29),
1887

Contract for Roofing Troyes Cathedral (11 October 1390)

Payment for work relating to the supply and use of building materials was the subject of very stringent contractual points.

Jehan Nepveu, called the slater [Escaillon], living in Reims, and his brother Colart, living in Troyes… recognized that they have entered into contract with venerable and discreet persons the dean and chapter of the church of Troyes to cover the roof of their church from the great pillars of the great crossing as far as the pillar which is beside the well…and they should supply the slate and nails and put them to use, by contract for piecework [made with my lords] £350 t. [*livres tournois*].

… And the said worshipful persons [i.e., the dean and chapter] are, and will be held, responsible for delivering to them planks of wood in sufficient quantity for the said roofing; and in addition to pay them, for the above contract, three hundred and fifty *livres tournois* in money that is legal tender on the day; of this sum, the said brothers had and received from the said worshipful persons, through the masters of the ecclesiastical works, in the presence of the said jurors, one hundred *livres tournois*; the two hundred and fifty *livres* remaining will be paid to them by the said worshipful persons in the following way: that is, on the next feast day of St. Andrew the Apostle one hundred *livres tournois*, twenty days after the following Christmas another hundred *livres tournois*, and the fifty remaining *livres tournois* when they have finished the said roofing. Giving their word to the said jurors, under pain of arrest, of being put and kept in prison, and against a guarantee of all their goods and the goods of their heirs, movables and real estate, now and to come, submitting and giving as guarantee the said goods to the judgment and decree of our Lord the King, of his men and of all other men of justice, the said brothers have undertaken, each for all, to make, accomplish perfectly, finish, and

Making glass for stained-glass windows required large quantities of sand and powerful furnaces.

successfully conclude all the above-mentioned things and each of these things in the manner stated above, without any shortcoming, without deviation, or causing deviation, on pain of having to reimburse and pay in return all costs and damages which might arise or depend on this: The said brothers renouncing, in everything which touches this, all regional custom and practice, all resort to castellany and provostship, all appeals, all other opposition that could be made against these letters or against their terms, and renouncing any action declaring the general renunciation invalid.…

Bibliothèque de l'Ecole des Chartes,
1862; first paragraph translated by
Stephen Murray in *Building*
Troyes Cathedral, 1987

Report on the Abbey Church of St.-Ouen at Rouen (1440)

The four piers supporting the crossing tower of the abbey church of St.-Ouen were giving cause for concern. In this detailed report, the architect, Colin de Berneval, successor to his father Alexandre, was relieved of all responsibility for the problem.

Below is the report of Simon Le Noir and Jehan Wyllemer, masters of the works in masonry and carpentry of our Lord the King in the bailiwick of Rouen, of Jehanson Salvart, master of works of the cathedral church of Our Lady at Rouen and of the said town, of Jehan Rouxel, juror of our Lord the King, and of Pierre Bense, master masons, all of whom have said and signified to the reverend father in God my lord the abbot of St.-Ouen and to the prior, the bailiff, the overseer of the granary, to the master of ecclesiastical works of the said place of St.-Ouen, how dangerous their church is, in view of the great load that weighs on the four piers of the tower and on the four great transverse arches.

These piers are not buttressed by their shifts and supports [?] on the side toward the crossing, and as a result they bulge out in those places and are very dangerous; for if the said piers or the great transverse arches should shift ever so slightly, the church would be in a position where the tower would collapse and the whole of the choir would follow.

To avert this danger, the said masters and workmen unanimously advise that as quickly as possible and without any interruption the shifts and supports [?] of the crossing, on which work has already begun, should be completed, so that the piers of the tower, the transverse arches, and the abutting piers should all be made secure, being linked more strongly together.

In order to be able to carry out this reinforcement rapidly, the masters and workmen named above declare that it would be wise to sell or to pawn chalices or objects of value to get money so that work could begin at once, and the church might be made safe; the which church is at the present moment in very great danger.

The master of the works, hearing the said report, instantly asked the said masters and workmen to put this report in writing on a sheet of parchment and sign it with their signatures or the seals which they used in their royal offices; and in the presence of my lord the abbot, of the prior, of the bailiff, of the overseer of the granary and of the said masters, he resigned the office of the works, so that if the church was not made safe and some disaster occurred, no one could turn against him or say that it was in some way his fault.

Present at this report was Colin de Berneval, appointed by my lord the abbot and by the monks named above to be the worker in masonry for their church in the future, as his father, the late Alexandre de Berneval, had been in his time. The said Colin de Berneval asked if he could hold in his possession a copy of the said report, for his indemnity in the future. This was done on Monday the twenty-third day of January, in the year of Grace 1440.

Bibliothèque de l'Ecole des Chartes, 1862

Building Techniques

Architects, who realized the extent of their abilities in the first third of the 11th century, proved to be not only great creative artists but also remarkable technicians. They had to devise new solutions to overcome difficulties. Very soon some of them began to produce "expertises," or professional assessments.

St.-Guy Cathedral, Prague.

Reconstruction of Cambrai Cathedral (*Gestum Pontificum Cameracensium*, 1023–30)

Like all the patrons of his generation, Gérard I, Bishop of Cambrai, tried to force the hand of fate.

The Lord Bishop Gérard first entered the town. When he saw that the buildings of the monastery of St. Mary were as small as they were decrepit, and he suspected their ancient walls were cracking, he swiftly conceived the project of putting them into a more satisfactory state, if only he were given the necessary time, with the help of God. But he could not undertake the project before the year of the Incarnation 1023…because he was prevented…by internal as well as external conflict. But then, trusting in divine mercy and reassured by the prayers of many of the faithful whom he had taken into his confidence, he gave orders to demolish the old walls. Once the necessary funds were pledged, he devoted all his energy to reconstructing a building that presented such great difficulties, for he had a fear of leaving the work unfinished, either because death might overtake him, or because some other reason might hinder him from completing it. In this respect, he realized that among the obstacles that might delay the project he had at heart, none was more difficult to overcome than the slowness of the transport of columns, cut a long way from the town, almost at the thirtieth milestone. And so he prayed Divine Mercy grant him assistance nearer at hand. One day while riding his horse, he explored the hidden depths of the earth in many surrounding places. At last, with the help of God who never fails those who put their trust in Him, he had a trench dug in the village that has always been known as Lesdain, four miles from the town, and found stone suitable for the columns. And this was not the only place: on digging nearer, to be precise on the estate [*villa*] of Nigella [Noyelles], he was pleased to find good quality stones of another kind. Giving thanks to God for this find, he devoted all his zeal to this pious work. And to cut short the story, in the space of seven years, with the help of Divine Mercy, he brought this huge work to its conclusion, that is in the year of the Incarnation of Our Lord 1030.

Victor Mortet,
Recueil de Textes Relatifs à l'Histoire de l'Architecture…, 1911

Construction of the Castle of Ardres, Near St.-Omer (*Chronicle of Lambert of Ardres*, 1060)

All construction involves destruction. In this case a group of buildings was moved from one place to another.

How Arnould, seneschal of Eustace, count of Boulogne, had all his buildings at Selnesse transported to the tall keep at Ardres. Arnould, seneschal of Eustace, count of Boulogne, seeing that everything smiled upon him and turned to his advantage, almost as he wished, had a sluice-gate made in a marsh in the neighborhood of Ardres almost a stone's throw from a mill, and then a second sluice. Between the two, in the middle of the marsh, which was deep, muddy and copiously filled with water, extending almost to the foot of a hill, he fortified a very high motte or "keep" that rose above a line of defense [*in*

munitionis signum] and above a dike. And from what the inhabitants say, a tame bear…transported the materials intended for the keep of this fortress between the hill [*altitudo*] and the motte. It is said that in a hiding place perfectly concealed within this dike a good-luck amulet was hidden, to remain there for ever; it was a lump of very pure gold. Arnould had the periphery of the outer fortification surrounded by a very solid ditch, the mill being included within the fortification. Soon, in accordance with his father's old plan, he had all the buildings at Selnesse pulled down and destroyed, then he had the keep at Ardres equipped with a bridge, gateways, and all the necessary buildings. From this day, once the vast residence of Selnesse had been demolished and razed to the ground and all its buildings dismantled and moved to Ardres, the very memory of Selnesse disappeared with its castle; so that first at Ardres and then everywhere, Arnould became known as the protector and lord of Ardres.

Victor Mortet,
Recueil de Textes Relatifs à l'Histoire de l'Architecture…, 1911

The Rebuilding of Canterbury Cathedral by William of Sens (*Chronicle of Gervase of Canterbury*)

In 1174 the whole east end of Canterbury Cathedral was destroyed by fire. It was witnessed by one of the monks, called Gervase. His account of the rebuilding, over the next ten years, included in his history of the archbishopric, is the most complete, most vivid, and most informative of all the documents on medieval architecture that have come down to us.

Meantime the brotherhood sought counsel as to how and in what manner the burnt church might be repaired, but without success; for the columns of the church, commonly termed the *pillars*, were exceedingly weakened by the heat of the fire, and were scaling in pieces and hardly able to stand, so that they frightened even the wisest out of their wits.

French and English artificers were therefore summoned, but even these differed in opinion. On the one hand, some undertook to repair the aforesaid columns without mischief to the walls above. On the other hand, there were some who asserted that the whole church must be pulled down if the monks wished to exist in safety. This opinion, true as it was, excruciated the monks with grief, and no wonder, for how could they hope that so great a work should be completed in their days by any human ingenuity.

However, amongst the other workmen there had come a certain William of Sens, a man active and ready, and as a workman most skillful both in wood and stone. Him, therefore, they retained, on account of his lively genius and good reputation, and dismissed the others. And to him, and to the providence of God was the execution of the work committed.

And he, residing many days with the monks and carefully surveying the burnt walls in their upper and lower parts, within and without, did yet for some time conceal what he found necessary to be done, lest the truth should kill them in their present state of pusillanimity.

But he went on preparing all things that were needful for the work, either of himself or by the agency of others. And

The choir of Canterbury Cathedral.

when he found that the monks began to be somewhat comforted, he ventured to confess that the pillars rent with the fire and all that they supported must be destroyed if the monks wished to have a safe and excellent building. At length they agreed, being convinced by reason and wishing to have the work as good as he promised, and above all things to live in security; thus they consented patiently, if not willingly, to the destruction of the choir.

And now he addressed himself to the procuring of stone from beyond the sea. He constructed ingenious machines for loading and unloading ships, and for drawing cement and stone. He delivered molds for shaping the stones to the sculptors who were assembled, and diligently prepared other things of the same kind. The choir thus condemned to destruction was pulled down, and nothing else was done in this year.

As the new work is of a different fashion from the old, it may be well to describe the old work first and then the new. Edmer, the venerable singer, in his Opuscula, describes the ancient church built in the Roman manner, which Archbishop Lanfranc, when he came to the See, utterly destroyed, finding it in ashes. For Christ Church is recorded to have suffered thrice from fire; first, when the blessed martyr Elfege was captured by the Danes and received the crown of martyrdom; secondly, when Lanfranc, abbot of Caen, took the rule of the church of Canterbury; thirdly, in the days of Archbishop Richard and Prior Odo.… Leaving out, therefore, all that is not absolutely necessary, let us boldly prepare for the destruction of

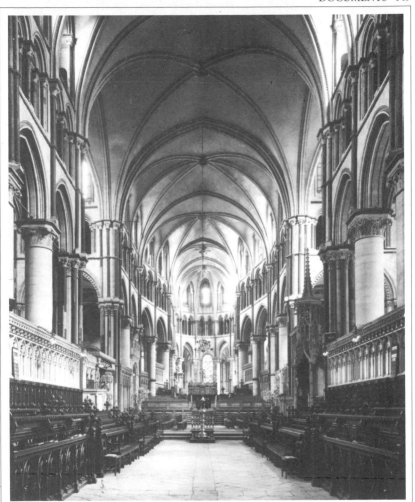

this old work and the marvellous building of the new, and let us see what our master William has been doing in the meanwhile.

The master began, as I stated long ago, to prepare all things necessary for the new work, and to destroy the old. In this way the first year was taken up. In the following year, that is after the feast of St. Bertin (Sept. 5, 1175) before the winter, he erected four pillars, that is, two on each side, and after the winter (1176) two more were placed, so that on each side were three in order, upon which and upon the exterior wall of the aisles he framed seemly arches and a vault, that is three [bays] on each side.... In the third year (1176/7) he placed two pillars on each side, the two extreme ones of which he decorated with marble columns placed around them, and because at that place the choir and [transepts] were to meet, he constituted these principal pillars. To which, having added the keystones and the vault, he intermingled the lower triforium from the great tower to the aforesaid pillars, that is, as far as the [transept], with many marble columns. Over which he adjusted another triforium of the other materials, and also the upper windows. And in the next place, three [bays] of the great vault, from the tower, namely, as far as the [transept]. All which things appeared to us and to all who saw them, incomparable and most worthy of praise. And at so glorious a beginning we rejoiced and conceived good hopes to the end, and provided for the acceleration of the work with diligence and spirit. Thus was the third year occupied and the beginning of the fourth.

In the summer (1178), commencing from the cross[ing], he erected ten pillars, that is, on each side five. Of which the first two were ornamented with marble columns to correspond with the other two principal ones. Upon these ten he placed the arches and vaults. And having, in the next place, completed on both sides the triforia and upper windows, he was, at the beginning of the fifth year, in the act of preparing with machines for the turning of the great vault, when suddenly the beams broke under his feet, and he fell to the ground, stones and timbers accompanying his fall, from the height of the capitals of the upper vault, that is to say, of fifty feet. Thus sorely bruised by the blows from the beams and stones, he was rendered helpless alike to himself and for the work, but no other than himself was in the least injured. Against the master only was this vengeance of God or spite of the devil directed.

The master, thus hurt, remained in his bed for some time under medical care in expectation of recovering, but was deceived in this hope, for his health amended not. Nevertheless, as the winter approached, and it was necessary to finish the upper vault, he gave the charge of the work to a certain ingenious and industrious monk, who was the overseer of the masons; an appointment whence much envy and malice arose, because it made this young man appear more skillful than richer and more powerful ones. But the master reclining in bed commanded all things that should be done in order. And thus was completed the [bay] between the four principal pillars. In the keystone of this [bay] the choir and [transepts] seem as it were to meet. Two [bays] on each side were formed before the winter; when the heavy rains beginning stopped the work. In these operations the fourth year was occupied and the beginning of the fifth. But on the eighth day from the said fourth year, on the ides of September, there happened an eclipse of the sun at about the sixth hour, and before the master's accident.

And the master, perceiving that he derived no benefit from the physicians, gave up the work, and crossing the sea returned to his home in France. And another succeeded him in charge of the works; William by name, English by

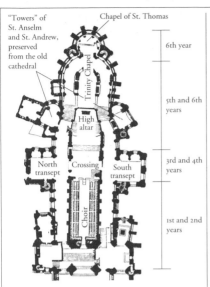

"Towers" of St. Anselm and St. Andrew, preserved from the old cathedral

Chapel of St. Thomas

Trinity Chapel

High altar

North transept

Crossing

South transept

Choir

6th year

5th and 6th years

3rd and 4th years

1st and 2nd years

Plan of the eastern part of Canterbury Cathedral showing the work carried out in successive years according to Gervase.

nation, small in body, but in workmanship of many kinds acute and honest. In the summer of the fifth year (1179) he finished the [transepts] on each side, that is, the south and the north, and [built the vault] which is above the great Altar, which the rains of the previous year had hindered, although all was prepared. Moreover he laid the foundation for the enlargement of the church at the eastern part, because a chapel of St. Thomas was to be built there....

Moreover, in the same summer, that is of the sixth year (1180), the outer wall round the chapel of St. Thomas, begun before the winter, was elevated as far as the turning of the vault. But the master had begun a tower at the eastern part outside the circuit of the wall as it were, the lower vault of which was completed before the winter.

The chapel of the Holy Trinity above mentioned was then levelled to the ground; this had hitherto remained untouched out of reverence to St. Thomas, who was buried in the crypt. But the saints who reposed in the upper part of the chapel were translated elsewhere, and lest the memory of what was then done should be lost, I will record somewhat thereof. On the eighth idus of July the altar of the Holy Trinity was broken up, and from its materials the altar of St. John the Apostle was made; I mention this lest the history of the holy stone should be lost....

It has been above stated, that after the fire nearly all the old portions of the choir were destroyed and changed into somewhat new and of a more noble fashion. The differences between the two works may now be enumerated. The pillars of the old and new work are alike in form and thickness but different in length. For the new pillars were elongated by almost twelve feet. In the old capitals the work was plain, in the new ones exquisite in sculpture. There the circuit of the choir had twenty-two pillars, here are twenty-eight. There the arches and everything else was plain, or sculptured with an axe and not with a chisel. But here almost throughout is appropriate sculpture. No marble columns were there, but here are innumerable ones. There, in the circuit around the choir, the vaults were plain, but here they are arch-ribbed and have keystones. There a wall set upon the pillars divided the crosses from the choir, but here the crosses are separated from the choir by no such partition, and converge together in one keystone, which is placed in the middle of the great vault which rests on the four principal pillars. There, there was a ceiling of wood decorated with excellent painting, but here is a vault beautifully constructed of stone and light tufa. There, was a single triforium, but here are two in the choir and a third in the aisle of the church. All which will be better understood from inspection than by any description.

This must be known, however, that the new work is higher than the old by so much as the upper windows of the body of the choir, as well as of its aisles, are raised above the marble tabling.

And as in future ages it may be doubtful why the breadth which was given to the choir next the tower should be so much contracted at the head of the church, it may not be useless to explain the causes thereof. One reason is, that the two towers of St. Anselm and St. Andrew, placed in the circuit on each side of the old church, would not allow the breadth of the choir to proceed in the direct line. Another reason is, that it was agreed upon and necessary that the chapel of St. Thomas should be erected at the head of the church, where the chapel of the Holy Trinity stood, and this was much narrower than the choir.

The master, therefore, not choosing to pull down the said towers, and being unable to move them entire, set out the breadth of the choir in a straight line, as far as the beginning of the towers. Then, receding slightly on either side from the towers, and preserving as much as he could the breadth of the passage outside the choir on account of the processions which were there frequently passing, he gradually and obliquely drew in his work, so that

from the opposite the altar, it might begin to contract, and from thence, at the third pillar, might be so narrowed as to coincide with the breadth of the chapel, which was named of the Holy Trinity. Beyond these, four pillars were set on the sides at the same distance as the last, but of a different form; and beyond these other four were arranged in a circle, and upon these the superposed work (of each side) was brought together and terminated. This is the arrangement of the pillars.

The outer wall, which extends from the aforesaid towers, first proceeds in a straight line, is then bent into a curve, and thus in the round tower the wall on each side comes together in one, and is there ended. All which may be more clearly and pleasantly seen by the eyes than taught in writing. But this much was said that the differences between the old and new work might be made manifest.

Now let us carefully examine what were the works of our mason in this seventh year (1181) from the fire, which, in short, included the completion of the new and handsome crypt, and above the crypt the exterior walls of the aisles up to their marble capitals. The windows, however, the master was neither willing nor able to turn, on account of the approaching rains. Neither did he erect the interior pillars. Thus was the seventh year finished, and the eighth begun.

In this eighth year (1182) the master erected eight interior pillars and turned the arches and the vault with the windows in the circuit. He also raised the tower up to the bases of the highest windows under the vault. In the ninth year (1183) no work was done for want of funds. In the tenth year (1184) the upper windows of the tower, together with the vault, were finished. Upon the pillars was placed a lower and an upper triforium.

Translated by Robert Willis in
The Architectural History of
Canterbury Cathedral, 1845

The "Expertise" of 1316 (on Chartres Cathedral)

The "Expertise" of 1316 is a report prepared by a group of architects—Pierre (i.e., Jean) de Chelles, master of the works of Paris, Nicolas des Chaumes, master of the king's works, and Jacques de Longjumeau, master carpenter of Paris— who were asked by the worried canons of Chartres to inspect the cathedral.

...My lords, we say to you that the four arches which help carry the vault are good and strong, and that the piers which carry the arches [are] good, and that the keystone which carries the summit[French *la clef qui porte la clef;* literally "the keystone that carries the keystone"] [of the vault is] good and strong; and it would not be necessary to remove more than half of your vault, at the place[s] where one will see what is needed. And we have noted that the scaffolding would move from above the tracery of the glass [French *enmerllement;* probably the assemblage of stones in the window tracery]; and this scaffolding can be used to help cover your rood screen and the people who will pass beneath it, and to hold the other scaffolds to be constructed in the vault, which one can see will be required and needed.

Here are the defects which are in the church of Notre-Dame at Chartres, seen by Master Pierre de Chelles, Master of

the Works of Paris; Master Nicolas des Chaumes, Master of the Works of our lord, the King; and Master Jacques de Longjumeau, Master Carpenter and officer of Paris, in the presence of Master Jean de Reate, canon of Chartres, originally from Italy; Master Simon, Carpenter; and Master Berthaud, officer of the aforementioned work, upon the order of the dean.

First: we have seen the vault of the crossing; repairs are necessary there; and if they are not undertaken very shortly, there could be great danger.

Item: we have seen the flying buttresses which abut the vaults; they need pointing up, and if this is not done at once, much damage may ensue.

Item: there are two piers which support the towers which need repairs.

Item: repairs are needed on the porch piers and a plank should be provided in each side opening to carry what lies above; and, on the outside, one of the jambs will be moved above the dado on the corner pier and the other jamb will be moved above a reworking of the fabric of the church; and the plank will have a support so as to reduce the strain; and this will be done with all the ties that are needed.

Item: we have seen and devised for Master Berthaud how he will [re]make the statue of the Magdalene where it now is, without moving it.

Item: we have looked at the great tower [the south tower] and see that it has real need of important repairs; for one of its sides is cracked and creviced and one of the turrets is broken and coming apart.

Item: the needs of the front portals follow—the coverings are broken and in pieces; wherefore it would be good to put an iron tenon in each to help hold

them up, and it should be well-seated so as to remove the danger.

Item: for the advantage of the church, we have noticed that the first scaffolding will be moveable from above the tracery of the windows so that the vault of the crossing may be redone.

Item: for the advantage of the church, we have noticed that the post that carries the little angel [the statue at the point of the roof covering the hemicycle] is all rotten and cannot join the other pier of the nave of the minster, for the pier of the minster is broken on the upper side of the assemblage of the beam; and if they want to work well,

The flying buttresses of Chartres Cathedral play a role that is primarily structural.

[the masters] will put two trusses with those which are on the chevet and will put the little angel on the second of these trusses; and the larger part of the beam, which is on the afore-mentioned ridge, could be put inside.

Item: the belfry, where the little saints are [the bells, which were usually given saints' names], is insufficient, for it is very old, as is the one where the large saints are; repairs to them are necessary at once.

Item: the roof of the minster needs four new tenons, [to replace those] which now are rotted at one end; they can be repaired, if you do not want to replace them, in the manner which we explained to your masters.

Translated by Robert Branner in *Chartres Cathedral*, 1969

Record of the Expertise at Troyes Cathedral (*Deliberations of the Chapter*, 1362)

The report on Troyes Cathedral reveals the structural problems for the architect.

This is the record of the visitation made by Master Pierre Faisant, mason, to the church of Troyes, in the year 1362, the Saturday after the feast day of St. Martin in the winter [12 November].

1. First, it is to be known that all the gutters of the low vaults are to be repointed, that is, [the gutters] around the choir of the said church.

2. Item, in several places the entablatures [balustrades] which are by the gargoyles are to be redone and re-erected.

3. Item, it is necessary to make 1 flying buttress by the chapel of my lord the bishop toward the court [south side of the choir] which will spring above the gutter and it is necessary that it [the flyer] should go as high above the rear tail as up to the base of the first pinnacle, and this only involves 1 single flying buttress.

4. Item, further, it seems to the said master who has looked at the new work of Master Jehan de Torvoie…that there is no fault except that the flying buttresses are placed too high, that is to say the upper flying buttress, and it seems to him that it is necessary to demolish the said work to the height of the pinnacles which rise from the angles, and [he] is for saving the [old] masonry completely throughout, and to do this and to put things right according to his profession will easily cost 250 florins.

5. Item, further, another thing, that there is a problem with the new flying buttress toward the house of the great archdeacon [north side of the choir], and he will show it, if need be, for, if the work is augmented with plaster and cement, it is not at all adequate. [He] says on this oath that although it might be uglier, it would not be any less strong or less worthy on that account.

6. Item, it seems that the pillars of the balustrade of the high gutters [of the clerestory wall] are fragmented and without cement and the [rain] water is running down the walls.

7. Item, in several places, that is to say in the joints in the passageways, the [rain] water is running down through the walls, and this must be remedied.

8. Item, the four gutters of the bell tower need to be fixed, that is at the joints above the flying buttresses, there is a major defect and it should be remedied.

9. And the said masters are at your disposal to be your own workers, if necessary.

Translated by Stephen Murray in *Building Troyes Cathedral*, 1987

Report on the Building of Milan Cathedral

Milan Cathedral was begun soon after 1386. It was on a vast scale, and the Lombard architects (called "the Masters" in the following document) found themselves out of their depth. In 1399 a Frenchman, Jean Mignot, was put in charge and made serious criticisms. The architects attempted to answer them, in vain.

1400 Sunday, 25 January. Master Jean Mignot has stated to the council here present that he has given in writing to the said council a note computing to date all the reasons and every motive which lead him to say that the aforesaid work lacks strength, and he does not wish to give other reasons.

Final statements were given by aforesaid Master Jean on the 25th day of January.

Master Jean Mignot points out to you excellent lords of the workshop council of the Milanese church with respect and pure truth that as he had demonstrated in writing elsewhere and among other matters, the defects of said church, he reiterates and affirms that all the buttresses around the church are neither strong nor able to sustain the weight which rests upon them, since they ought in every case to be three times the thickness of one pier in the interior of the church. The Masters reply:

Concerning the first statement, they say that all the buttresses of said church, are strong and capable of sustaining

The nave of Milan Cathedral.

their weight and many times more, for many reasons, since one braccio of our marble and *saritium*, whatever its width, is as strong as two braccia of French stone or of the French church which he gives to the aforesaid masters as an example. Therefore they say that if aforesaid buttresses are one-and-a-half times [the size]—and they are—of the piers in the interior of the church, that they are strong and correctly conceived, and if they were larger they would darken said church because of their projection, as at the church in Paris, which has buttresses of Master Jean's type, and since they can be an obstruction [there are] other reasons.

Moreover, he [Mignot] says that four towers were begun to support the crossing-tower of said church, and there are no piers nor any foundation capable of sustaining said towers, and if the church were to be made with said towers in this position it would infallibly fall. Concerning the claims, however, which were made by certain ignorant people, surely through passion, that pointed vaults are stronger and exert less thrust than round, and moreover concerning other matters, proposals were made in a fashion more willful than sound; and what is worse, it was objected that the science of geometry should not have a place in these matters, since science is one thing and art another. Said Master Jean says that art without science is nothing [*ars sine scientia nihil est*], and that whether the vaults are pointed or round, they are worthless unless they have a good foundation, and nevertheless, no matter how pointed they are,

they have a very great thrust and weight.

Whereupon they [the Masters] say that the towers which they wanted to make are for many reasons and causes [desirable]. Namely, in the first place, to integrate aforesaid church and transept so that they correspond to a rectangle according to the demands of geometry, but beyond this, for the strength and beauty of the crossing-tower. To be sure, as if as a model for this, the Lord God is seated in Paradise in the center of the throne, and around the throne are the four Evangelists according to the Apocalypse, and these are the reasons why they were begun. And although two piers of each sacristy are not founded, but begin at ground level, the church is truly strong nevertheless for these reasons, that there are projections upon which the said piers stand, and the said projections are of large stones and joined with iron dowels as was said above other statements, and that the weight on these three [*sic*] towers falls evenly on their square, and they will be built properly and strong, and what is vertical cannot fall; therefore they say that they are strong in themselves, and for that reason will give strength to the crossing-tower, which is enclosed in the center of those towers. Therefore said church is truly strong.

Moreover he [Mignot] recognizes that their premises are willfully conceived, nor do those who disagree wish to give in to the right and the betterment of said church and workshop, but want to win their case either for their own profit or from fear, or else from obstinacy, since they would like to continue in spite of defects. For this reason said Master Jean requests that four or six or twelve of the better engineers who are expert in these matters might be brought together, either from Germany, England, or France, otherwise said work will certainly fall, which would be a great loss in every way....

Whereupon they [the Masters] say and reply in the same statement, that where it says that the science of geometry should not have a place in these [matters], the above-mentioned say: if he [Mignot] invokes, as it were, the rules of geometry, Aristotle says that the movement of man in space which we call locomotion is either straight or circular or a mixture of the two. Likewise the same [writer] says elsewhere that every body is perfected in three

[ways], and the movement of this very church rises *ad triangulum* as has been determined by other engineers. So they say that all [the measurements] are in a straight line, or an arch, therefore it is concluded that what has been done, has been done according to geometry and to practice, and even he [Mignot] has said that science without art is nothing; concerning art, however, replies have been made already in other statements.

In February 1400 a conference was called, at which several notable architects from France, Italy, and Germany gave their opinions.

1400—21 February. On 21 February 1400, in his palace there came before the most reverend Archbishop of Milan numerous deputies and members of the council of the Cathedral, and Simonetus Negrus, Johannes Sanomerius, and Mermetus de Sabandia [Savoy], all three French engineers and [they] were queried on the questions set forth in writing below as to what they would say and decide under oath since they are in transit to Rome.

First it was asked on this question by the above-mentioned lords if it seemed to them that this church was adequately founded to sustain and carry the weight belonging to said church.

We the aforesaid engineers and masons say that we have seen and reviewed all of said church, and especially we have seen the foundations of two piers exposed, which two piers should sustain and abut the apse of said church, and are inadequately and poorly founded. And one of these is more than a foot at fault inside the work, and of poor material. All the piers of said church both inside and outside are to be reviewed

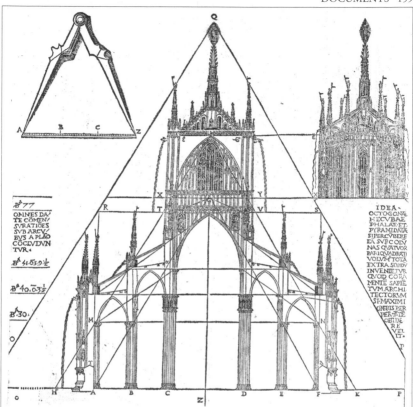

Section through Milan Cathedral analyzed according to the medieval proportional system called *ad triangulum*, which was advocated by Paul Mignot.

down to the lowest base and all those which were badly founded as are the aforementioned, are to be refounded of large blocks of well-laid stone, and their bedding should be well leveled and planed and joined, and buttressed by dovetailing into the other foundations well inside, and built in with a mortar bath. These foundations should be made two braccia or more beyond the plumb line of the bases of the piers, coming to one braccio at the surface by a setback.

Furthermore, it was asked and the question was put if the aforementioned two piers outside the apse of said church are strong enough to sustain and buttress against all its weight.

We state that if one founded two piers for carrying two flying buttresses, that the church would be made stronger....

Furthermore, it was asked and the question was put if all the other piers of said church seemed to us to be good.

We state that if they were to be made now they could be made better.

Furthermore it was asked if all the aforesaid piers could carry and transmit their loads as they are (now).

We reply that it seems so to us providing a good mason were available to change the mouldings and load-bearing members above the capitals, and to make this moulding proper and lighter, as it should be, since some of these piers are not well aligned....

Furthermore we note that there are cracks and holes cut through from the circular openings [probably stairwells] of the corner pier of the sacristies of this cathedral to carry off the rain water that is shed from the roofs of the sacristies and chapels, and this is unsound. It is necessary that they be closed and cemented up and that additional, new gargoyles be made....

(Signed) Symonetus Nigrus, Johannes Sanomerius, and Mermetus de Sabaudia.

1400—8 May. In the name of God and the Virgin Our Lady Saint Mary, in the year 1400 on the 8th of May. I, Bertolino of Novara, who have been sent by the illustrious and most high prince, my lord, the Duke, for certain views and disagreements brought up by some of the masters in the construction and commission of the church of our lady, St. Mary, which disagreements and opinions the overseers of the said construction have given me in writing, and I have seen and examined, and besides, I have been with the masters and engineers who are at present on this said construction, to see the disagreements with my own eyes from every angle. And besides this looking, I had the foundations of the said church dug into at certain points to see the said

foundations, so as to be clearer about the doubts brought up about the construction. Briefly answering, I said that the church should have had a truer proportion around the foundations, and in certain other places above ground. But it is not to be scorned on that account, in fact it is to be praised for a most beautiful big building, but in my opinion it would have to have an addition made for permanent strengthening as follows:

First, because the buttresses of the body of the church are not as large as is needed, considering the breadth and height of the said church, the first nave should be reduced to the form of chapels with partitions between one chapel and another, with some openings through which one could see the Host from either side of the church. By doing this the greatest strength would result in the other three naves, on account of these thrown arches, it would have a sounder base, and the body of the church would be beautiful and more wisely rational because it would match the size of the crossing.

Further, there would be need to make a chapel at the apse of the church toward the cemetery, which chapel would be attached to those two buttresses on the right side, making it as small as possible and not damaging anything already built, and this chapel would result in more strength, and in this area could be placed that tomb which it is said my lord, the Duke, wishes to make, and with the tomb installed in this place it could be located straighter, because the choir would turn out larger.

Master Bernardo of Venice, Master Bertolino of Novara, from Elizabeth G. Holt, ed., *A Documentary History of Art*, 1957–8

Contract for Building the Nave of Fotheringay Church

In the 15th century Fotheringay church, in Northamptonshire, was rebuilt to serve as the church of a college founded by one of the sons of Edward III. As was normal, the choir was built first. In 1435 it was time to start on the nave, and a contract was drawn up with a builder named William Horwood, who was told to follow the design of the choir that had already been built (but which no longer exists).

This contract made between William Wolston, squire, Thomas Pecham, clerk, commissioners for the high and mighty prince, and my right dread lord, the Duke of York, on the first part, and William Horwood, free-mason, dwelling in Fotheringay, on the other part, witnesses that the same William Horwood has granted and undertaken, and by this same has contracted, granted and undertaken to make up a new nave of a church joining to the choir, of the college of Fotheringay, of the same height and breadth that the said choir is; and in length eighty feet from the said choir downward, within walls a meter-yard [thick] a meter-yard of England, counted always as three feet. And in this covenant, the said William Horwood shall also make well all the ground work of the said nave, and take it and excavate it at his own cost, and as slowly and as adequately as it ought to be, overseen by masters of the same craft. The material that belongs to such a work is sufficiently provided for him at my said lord's cost. And to the said nave he shall make two aisles, and do the ground work and excavation of them in the aforesaid manner, both the aisles to be in accordance with the height and breadth of the aisles of said choir, and the height of the aforesaid nave; the ground of the same nave and aisles to be made within the end with rough stone under the ground tablestones; and for the ground stones b...ments [*sic*]; and all the remainder of the said nave and aisles to the full height of said choir all made with clean-hewn ashlar in the outer side to the full height of the said choir. And all the inner side to be of rough-stone, except that the bench-table-stones, the sills of the windows, the pillars and capitals that the arches and pendants rest upon, shall all be of freestone wrought truly and duly as it ought to be.

And in each aisle shall be windows of free-stone, agreeing in all points to the windows of the said choir, but they shall have no bowtels at all. And in the west end of either of the said aisles, he shall make a window of four lights, agreeing with the windows of the said aisles. And to either aisle shall be as square embattaillment of free-stone through out, and both the ends embattailled butting upon the steeple. And either of the said aisles shall have six mighty buttresses of free-stone, clean-hewn; and every buttress finished with a pinnacle, agreeing in all points to the pinnacles of the said choir, save only that the buttress of the nave shall be larger, stronger and mightier than the buttress of the said choir.

And the clerestory, both within and without, shall be made of clean ashlar grounded upon ten mighty pillars, with four responds; that is to say two above joining the choir, and two beneath joining to the end of the said nave. And to the two responds of the said choir shall be two perpeyn-walls joining of free-stone, clean wrought: that is to say, one on either side of the middle choir door. And in either wall, three lights, and piscinas on either side of the wall, which shall serve for four altars, that is to say one on either side of the middle door of the said choir and one on either side of the said aisles.

And in each of the said aisles shall be five arches above [sic] the steeple, and above every arch a window and every window to be of four lights, agreeing in all points to the windows of the clerestory of the said choir. And either of the said aisles shall have six mighty arches butting on either side to the clerestory, and two mighty arches butting on either side to the said steeple, agreeing with the arches of the said choir, both in table-stones and crestis, with a square embattaillment thereupon....

And to the west end of the said nave shall be a steeple standing [high above] the church upon three strong and mighty arches vaulted with stone. The said steeple shall have in length eighty feet after the meter-yard of three feet to the yard, above the ground from the table-stones, and [measure] twenty feet square within the walls, the walls being six foot thick above the said ground table-stones. And to the height of the said nave [of the church], it shall be square, with a large door, which shall be in the west end of the same steeple.

And when the said steeple comes to the height of the said battlement, then it shall be changed and turned in eight panes and at every angle, a buttress finished with a pinnacle agreeing to the pinnacles of the said choir and nave; the said chapell [to be] embattailled with a large square embattaillment. And above the door of the said steeple, a window

rising in height as high as the great arch of the steeple and in breadth as wide as the nave will come out to be. And in the said steeple will be two floors, and above each floor eight clerestory set in the middle of the wall, each window of three lights, and all the outer side of the steeple of clean wrought free-stone; and the inner side of rough stone. And in said steeple shall be a stair-way, serving up to the said nave, aisles and choir, both beneath and above....

And for all the work that is devised and rehearsed in this same agreement, my said Lord of York shall find the carriage and materials, that is to say, stone, lime, sand, ropes, bolts, ladders, timber, scaffolds, machines, and all kinds of materials that belong to the said work, by which the work will be well, truly, and duly made and finished in the manner as it is above devised and declared. The said William Horwood shall have of my said lord, three hundred pounds Sterling; of which sum he shall be paid in the manner as it shall be declared hereafter; that is to say, when he has excavated the ground of said church, aisles, buttresses, porches, and steeple, hewn and set his ground table-stones, and his string-courses and the wall thereto within and without as it ought to be well and duly made, then he shall have six pounds, thirteen shillings, four pence. And when the said William Horwood has set one foot above the ground table-stone, also the outer side as well as the inner side throughout all the said work, then he shall have payment of a hundred pounds Sterling. And so for every foot of the said work, after it be fully wrought and set as it ought to be and as it is above devised, until it comes to the full height of the highest pinnacles and battlement of the said nave, hewing, setting, raising [the tower] of the steeple after it has passed the highest embattaillment of the said nave, he shall have but thirty shilling Sterling, until it be fully ended and completed in the manner as it is above directed.

And when all the work above rehearsed and devised is fully finished, as it ought to be and as it is above agreed to and devised between the said commissioners and the said William, then the said William Horwood shall have full payment of the three pounds Sterling if any be due or left unpaid thereof to him.... And if it be that the said William Horwood not make full payment to all or any of his workmen, then the clerk of the work shall pay him in his presence and stop as much from the said William Horwood's hand as the payment amounts to that shall be due to the workmen.

And during all the said work, the setters shall be chosen and taken by those that shall have the control and supervision of the said work for my said lord. They are to be paid by the hand of the said William Horwood, in the form and manner above written and devised. And if it should be that the said William Horwood will complain and say at any time that two setters of any of them, be not profitable nor adequate workmen for my lord's profit, then with the oversight of the master-masons of the country they shall be judged. And if they be found faulty or unable, then they shall be changed and others taken and chosen by such as shall have control of the said work by my said lord's order and command.

And if it be that the said William Horwood makes not end of the said work within reasonable time, which

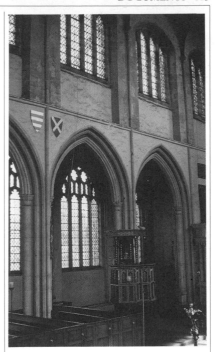

The nave of Fotheringay Church.

shall be set clearly by my said lord, or by his counsel in form and manner as is above written and devised in these same agreements, then he shall yield his body to prison at my lord's will, and all his movable goods and heritances at my said lord's disposition and order.

In witness, & the said commissioners, as [well as] the said William Horwood have set their seals interchangeably to these present contracts, the XXIVth day of September, the XIIIth year of the reign of our sovereign lord King Henry the Sixth, after the conquest of England.

from Douglas Knoop and G. P. Jones,
The Medieval Mason, 1933

Machines

Texts concerning the making of machines are less numerous than those on architecture.

Construction of a Crane at Arles (Notary's Draft, 1459)

In the year shown above [1459], on the seventh day of the month of June. It is hereby notified to everyone, etc.:

That the Reverend Master Alziarius Bartholomei, master of theology, venerable prior of the convent of the Order of Preachers [i.e., Dominicans] at Arles, has made payment and disbursement to Master Guyot Perissis, building timber merchant, living in Arles, here present, etc., for him to construct from new and to make in good building timber, new and suitable, a good and fitting crane able to carry and to support a weight of one hundred Arles quintals, with the object of erecting the new church which the said convent is having built and constructed in praise and honor of God and the glorious Virgin Mary of Succor, begun on the flank or side of the church of the said convent, and in order to raise the

A crane inspired by a war machine, by Mariano Taccola, a 15th-century Sienese "engineer."

stones and other materials necessary to the construction of this church, with and under the clauses set out below.

And that in the first place, the said Master Guyot is held and obliged to build well and construct in due form the said crane, to have it assembled and placed on the site of the said church, during the length of the present month of June, and to make it of a height of eight rods, in such a way that it can be used both inside and outside; and that the said lord prior must at his own cost and expense maintain and clean the site where the said crane is to be installed. It has been agreed similarly that the said lord prior must at the expense and cost of his convent have all the pieces of ironwork necessary for the said crane, and must execute all repairs necessary to these same pieces of ironwork at the expense of the said convent.

It has been similarly agreed that the said lord prior or his convent shall give in payment to the said Master Guyot for the said crane in such fashion as he has promised to make it, for the timber as well as for his own labor, forty-eight florins, that is to say two florins at once as deposit and payment, and the remaining forty-six florins to be paid within fifteen days, once the said crane has been manufactured and tried out [*probatum*], to see whether it is suitable or not [*si fuerit sufficiens*], from the day when it will have been installed on its site: the which two florins as deposit and payment, to be deducted from the said forty-eight florins, the said Master Guyot has acknowledged to hold and to have received from the said lord prior, with no exceptions etc....

Sealed at Arles in the said convent, in the cloister range next to the library, in presence of the witnesses: Pierre Jacquin, boatman, Master Byon Alvernhas, mason, citizens of Arles living there, and myself, Bernard Pangonis, notary, etc....

B. Montagnes
Architecture Dominicaine en Provence
1979

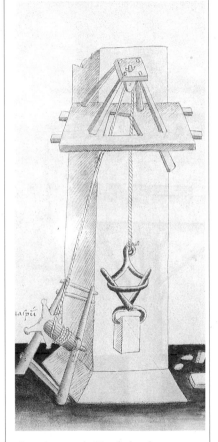

Another crane by Taccola, based on an invention by his friend the architect Filippo Brunelleschi.

Thirty-One Great Cathedrals

BRITAIN

Bristol: Unique in Britain as a "hall" church, the aisles as high as the central vessel, with buttresses in the form of bridges across the aisles carrying the thrust of the vault. Late 13th century.

Canterbury: East end rebuilt in the late 12th century. Largely French in style, but uses English Purbeck marble. Retains nearly all its stained glass. The nave was rebuilt in Perpendicular style in the 14th century.

Durham: The most complete survivor from the period when all English cathedrals were rebuilt following the Norman Conquest. Has its original nave, transept, and choir, covered with the earliest high rib vault in Europe. 11th–12th centuries.

Ely: Romanesque nave and transepts, 12th century. Octagon over the crossing built in the Decorated period, mid 14th century, with unique use of diagonal light.

Exeter: Built in the late 13th–early 14th century, a period when England's Decorated style led the rest of Europe. Intricately patterned rib vault and windows with curvilinear tracery.

Gloucester: Choir and south transept of the Romanesque church remodeled in the 14th century, originating the Perpendicular style, straight tracery covering the walls and expanding into the vault.

Lincoln: Rebuilding begun a few years after Canterbury, using the same elements but no longer in a French way.

Peterborough: Romanesque nave (12th century) and Romanesque painted ceiling. Characterized by extreme length.

Salisbury: Stylistically the most consistent of English cathedrals, built within forty years (1220–60), with the tower and spire a little later.

Westminster Abbey: Begun by Henry III (mid-13th century) as the coronation and burial church of the English kings. The most French of English great churches; the series of royal tombs from Henry III to Elizabeth I makes it of unique historical interest. The early-16th-century Henry VII Chapel is the last and most ingenious of fan-vaulted structures.

Wells: Begun at the same time as Canterbury and shares many of its features. The Decorated retrochoir (late 13th century) is a fascinating vista of complex spaces.

FRANCE

All the following were begun from 1150 to 1250

Amiens: Follows the pattern of Reims, its two-towered facade decorated with fine sculpture.

Beauvais: The most ambitious of all Gothic cathedrals, with a vault higher than any other—it was in fact too ambitious: The vault collapsed and had to be rebuilt, and the cathedral never progressed beyond the crossing.

Bourges: The most original in design. It has double aisles, the nave arcade being so high that the inner aisle has a complete three-story elevation (arcade, triforium, clerestory) of its own.

Chartres: Best preserved of all medieval cathedrals. Elaborate sculptural ensembles on the west front and both transept porches. A dazzling display of stained glass.

Laon: Notable especially for its twin-towered west front with figures of oxen, drawn by Villard de Honnecourt.

Paris, Notre-Dame: Set the pattern for cathedrals in the Ile-de-France: double aisles, four-story elevation, chevet with radiating chapels, two-tower facade, quadripartite vaults.

Reims: Coronation church of the French kings with notable sculpture and the earliest use of bar tracery.

GERMANY AND CENTRAL EUROPE

Cologne: Started in the 13th century. A French cathedral on German soil. Unfinished in the Middle Ages, finished according to the original design in the 19th century.

Prague: Begun by a French architect in the 14th century and taken over by a German. As at Cologne, its nave was not built until the 19th century.

Ulm: Started in the 14th century. Specifically German in having a single west tower and spire, also completed in the 19th century.

ITALY

Florence: Arcade arches even broader than Siena (nave of four bays only), 14th century. Brunelleschi's octagonal dome of the 1420s is the last great work of the Italian Middle Ages and the first of the Renaissance.

Milan: Begun in the 13th century, finished in the 19th. The only Italian cathedral comparable to the Gothic of the north, and partly designed by northern masters. On a vast scale, of white marble with a wealth of figure sculpture, curvilinear tracery, and pinnacles.

Monreale: Sicilian Romanesque, late 12th century. Union of Byzantine and Western influences, with marble columns, a wooden roof, and mosaic decoration.

Pisa: Tuscan Romanesque, 11th century. Exterior covered with dwarf galleries on miniature columns.

Siena: Has the broad arches of Italian Gothic, 13th–14th centuries, and the local specialty of horizontal banding in white and green. Crossing surmounted by hexagonal dome.

SPAIN

Burgos: The west towers and spires were designed by a master mason whose family came from Cologne. 13th–15th centuries.

Gerona: Choir begun as a cathedral with nave and aisles, but in the 15th century the whole nave was thrown into one space (no arcades) covered by the widest Gothic vault in the world.

León: Basically French Gothic. Retains much stained glass. 13th–14th century.

Santiago de Compostela: Built as the focus of a pilgrimage. Belongs to a French church type, with barrel vault and no clerestory. 12th century.

Seville: Embodies the Spanish characteristic of extreme width; covers the largest area of all medieval cathedrals. 15th century.

—Ian Sutton

Further Reading

ARCHITECTURE

Bony, Jean, *The English Decorated Style: Gothic Architecture Transformed*, Cornell University Press, Ithaca, 1979

Bony, Jean, *French Gothic Architecture of the 12th and 13th Centuries*, University of California Press, Berkeley, 1983

Frankl, Paul, *Gothic Architecture*, Penguin, Baltimore, 1962

Grodecki, Louis, *Gothic Architecture*, I. Mark Paris, trans., Abrams, New York, 1985

Harvey, John Hooper, *The Perpendicular Style*, Batsford, London, 1978

Webb, Geoffrey, *Architecture in Britain: The Middle Ages*, Penguin, Baltimore, 1956

White, John, *Art and Architecture in Italy, 1250 to 1400*, Penguin, Harmondsworth, England, 1987

Wilson, Christopher, *The Gothic Cathedral: The Architecture of the Great Church, 1130–1530*, Thames and Hudson, London, 1990

BUILDING TECHNIQUES

Coldstream, Nicola, *Masons and Sculptors*, British Museum Press, London, 1991

Fitchen, John, *The Construction of Gothic Cathedrals*, Clarendon, Oxford, 1961

Gille, Bertrand, *Engineers of the Renaissance*, MIT Press, Cambridge, Massachusetts, 1966

Gimpel, Jean, *The Cathedral Builders*, Teresa Waugh, trans., HarperCollins, New York, 1983

Harvey, John Hooper, *The Medieval Architect*, St. Martin's, New York, 1972

Knoop, Douglas, and G. P. Jones, *The Medieval Mason*, Barnes and Noble, New York, 1967

Murray, Stephen, *Building Troyes Cathedral*, Indiana University Press, Bloomington, 1987

Recht, Roland, *Les Bâtisseurs des Cathédrales Gothiques*, 1989

Salzman, Louis Francis, *Building in England Down to 1540*, Clarendon, Oxford, 1952

CRAFT

Binski, Paul, *Painters*, British Museum Press, London, 1991

Brown, Sarah, *Glass-Painters*, British Museum Press, London, 1991

Grodecki, Louis, and Catherine Brisac, *Gothic Stained Glass: 1200–1300*, Barbara Drake Boehm, trans., Cornell University Press, Ithaca, 1985

Harvey, John Hooper, *Medieval Craftsmen*, Drake, New York, 1975

GENERAL

Branner, Robert, *Chartres Cathedral*, Norton, New York, 1969

Clifton-Taylor, Alec, *The Cathedrals of England*, Thames and Hudson, London, 1986

Coulton, George Gordon, *Medieval Panorama: The English Scene from Conquest to Reformation*, University Press, Cambridge, England, 1939

Cowen, Painton, *Rose Windows*, Thames and Hudson, New York, 1990

Evans, Joan, *Life in Medieval France*, Humphrey Milford, London, 1925

Fagniez, Gustave, *Etudes sur l'Industrie et la Classe Industrielle à Paris au XIIIe et au XIV Siècles*, 1877

Favier, Jean, *The World of Chartres*, Abrams, New York, 1990

Huizinga, Johan, *The Waning of the Middle Ages*, E. Arnold, London, 1952

Loyn, H. R., ed., *The Middle Ages: A Concise Encyclopaedia*, Thames and Hudson, London, 1989

McEvedy, Colin, *The Penguin Atlas of Medieval History*, Penguin, Harmondsworth, England, 1961

Martindale, Andrew, *Gothic Art from the Twelfth to the Fifteenth Centuries*, Praeger, New York, 1967

Norman, Edward R., *The House of God: Church Architecture, Style, and History*, Thames and Hudson, New York, 1990

Southern, Richard William, *The Making of the Middle Ages*, Yale University Press, New Haven, 1953

TEXTS

Holt, Elizabeth G., ed., *A Documentary History of Art*, Doubleday, Garden City, New York, 1957–8

Mortet, Victor, *Recueil de Textes Relatifs à l'Histoire de l'Architecture . . . XIe–XIIe Siècles*, A. Picard et Fils, Paris, 1911

Mortet, Victor, and Paul Deschamps, *Recueil de Textes Relatifs à l'Histoire de l'Architecture . . . XIIe–XIIIe Siècles*, Editions Auguste Picard, 1929

Panofsky, Erwin, ed. and trans., *Abbot Suger on the Abbey Church of St.-Denis and Its Art Treasures*, Princeton University Press, Princeton, 1979

The Sketchbook of Villard de Honnecourt, Theodore Bowie, ed., Greenwood, Westport, Connecticut, 1982

Willis, Robert, *The Architectural History of Canterbury Cathedral*, 1845 (contains a translation of Gervase's account)

List of Illustrations

Index

Acknowledgments

The publishers would like to thank François Avril and Jean-Pierre Aniel of the manuscripts department of the Bibliothèque Nationale.

Photo Credits

Text Credits

Grateful acknowledgment is made for use of material from the following: The "Expertise" of 1316 (on Chartres Cathedral), translated by Robert Branner in Robert Branner, *Chartres Cathedral*, Thames and Hudson, 1969; used with the permission of Shirley Branner (pp. 153–5). Elizabeth G. Holt, *A Documentary History of Art*, 1957, copyright © 1947, 1957 Princeton University Press (pp. 156–60). *Bibliothèque de l'Ecole des Chartes*, 1862, translated by Stephen Murray in Stephen Murray, *Building Troyes Cathedral*, Indiana University Press, 1987, © 1987 by Stephen Murray (pp. 143–4, first paragraph). *Deliberations of the Chapter*, 1362, translated by Stephen Murray in Stephen Murray, *Building Troyes Cathedral*, Indiana University Press, 1987, © 1987 by Stephen Murray (pp. 155–6). *The Metrical Life of St. Hugh*, translated by Charles Gaston, The Honywood Press, 1986; reprinted with the permission of The Honywood Press, Lincoln, England (pp. 132–4)

Alain Erlande-Brandenburg, who studied at
the Ecole Nationale des Chartes, is the director of the
National Archives of France, director of studies at the Ecole
Pratique des Hautes Etudes, and professor of the history
of art at the Ecole des Chartes, all in Paris. He was
chief curator of the Musée National du Moyen Age, chief
curator of the Musée National de la Renaissance, of
which he was a founder, and assistant to the director of
the Musées de France (1987–91). He has gained an
international reputation for a number of important
publications on the Gothic era. He is responsible for an
enlightening work on the new conception of the history
of art: *La Cathédrale*, 1989. He is the president
of the Société Française d'Archéologie.

*To my colleagues at the Société Française d'Archéologie with
whom I have—over the past twenty-five years—discovered
the greatness and the beauty of medieval architecture.
In community of spirit.*

Translated from the French by Rosemary Stonehewer

Editor: Sharon AvRutick
Typographic Designer: Elissa Ichiyasu
Design Supervisor: Miko McGinty
Assistant Designer: Tina Thompson
Text Permissions: Neil Ryder Hoos

Library of Congress Catalog Card Number: 94–77944

ISBN 0–8109–2812–4

Copyright © 1993 Gallimard

English translation copyright © 1995 Harry N. Abrams, Inc., New York,
and Thames and Hudson Ltd., London

Published in 1995 by Harry N. Abrams, Inc., New York
A Times Mirror Company

All rights reserved. No part of the contents of this book may be reproduced
without the written permission of the publisher

Printed and bound in Italy by Editoriale Libraria, Trieste